SKINNY
SOUPS

SKINNY SOUPS

80 flavour-packed recipes of less than 300 calories

Kathryn Bruton

Photography by Laura Edwards

Kyle Books

To Dad

First published in Great Britain in 2016 by
Kyle Books, an imprint of Kyle Cathie Ltd
192–198 Vauxhall Bridge Road
London SW1V 1DX
general.enquiries@kylebooks.com
www.kylebooks.com

10 9 8 7 6 5 4 3 2

ISBN 978 0 85783 300 6

Project Editor: Claire Rogers
Copy Editor: Anne Newman
Designer: Louise Leffler
Photographer: Laura Edwards
Food Stylists: Annie Rigg and Kathryn Bruton
Prop Stylist: Liz Belton
Production: Nic Jones and Gemma John

A Cataloguing in Publication record for this title is
available from the British Library.

Colour reproduction by F1, London
Printed in Slovenia by DZS Grafik

Nutritional information key:
DF – dairy-free
GF – gluten-free
V – vegetarian
VE – vegan

contents

Introduction 6
Equipment 8
A Few Useful Notes 10
Store-cupboard Suggestions 11
Unusual Ingredients 12
Homemade Stocks and Pastes 14

Smooth Soups 20
Broths and Consommés 48
15-Minute Soups 76
Grains and Pulses 104
Superfood Soups 128

Suppliers 156
Index 157

introduction

I adore soup. It is the simplest of concepts with endless potential. Every culture has its own version, each as interesting and inspiring as the next. There is no limit to how healthy a soup can be and the recipes in this book showcase how it can be exciting and different, bursting with fantastic ingredients, flavours and textures, low in calories and high in nutritients – all at the same time. It is the epitome of food for mind, body and soul.

Everyone can make soup successfully. As with anything homemade, you can pack it with goodness. As well as being full of healthy ingredients, every recipe in this book is less than 300 calories per portion, and many are even less. No calorie-controlled meal should leave you hungry. Here you will find soups fit for a main meal, fantastically filling lunch options, breakfast bowls designed to positively kick-start your day and even delicious desserts, a testament to how creative this wonderful dish can be.

I love to play around with ideas, be creative and design imaginative and original dishes – you won't find any leek and potato soups in this book. Instead, I have used my imagination to create delicious, interesting recipes. The quest to pack each bowl with goodness and flavour is the backbone for each recipe, and I hope that you will feel inspired to cook soup bursting with flavours you either love or are interested to try.

This book is for everyone – those with and without food intolerances and those who eliminate certain food groups from their diet. Soups are often, by default, vegetarian, vegan, gluten- or dairy-free, and many of the recipes in this book are some, if not all, of the above. Where they are not a few simple changes will make them suitable for you in most cases.

The chapters have been organised to showcase soup's adaptability. Creamy creations make their way into the Smooth Soups chapter, some served simply, others adorned with exciting garnishes. My travels around South East Asia inspired many of the recipes in the Broths and Consommés chapter. The 15-Minute Soups chapter will hopefully help when you are constantly chasing your tail. Grains and Pulses take centre stage in their very own chapter, and the last chapter champions superfoods for a concentrated dose of nutrition.

Creating the recipes in this book has been one of my most interesting and exciting adventures – many happy months were spent consuming and being all-consumed by soup. I could carry on forever; such is the versatility of this humble dish – it has infinite possibilities. My adventure is finished and, in buying this book, you have begun yours. Every recipe is open to interpretation, ready for you to stamp with your personality, if you so wish. Whether you use these recipes as guide to eat healthier, aid weight loss or simply enjoy some delicious bowls, the only thing I ask is that you have fun doing it.

equipment

The beauty of soup is that it requires very little kitchen equipment and much of what you need will most likely be in your cupboards already. However, there are a few pieces that are particularly useful, and it may be worth investing in some of the items below to achieve the best possible results.

Blenders, hand-held stick blenders and food-processors

A blended soup is at its best when it is smooth like velvet. Specifically designed to deal with liquids, a blender gives soups a beautifully smooth and uniform consistency and is my weapon of choice. If you are planning to make a lot of soup, I would recommend investing in one of these.

A hand-held stick blender will also do the trick, although some vegetables such as broccoli, cauliflower and sweetcorn resist the smaller, less powerful blade, resulting in a somewhat grainy texture. If you already have a stick blender and would rather not invest in another piece of kitchen equipment, you can try passing the soup through a sieve after blending for a smoother consistency.

Food-processors pose much the same problem, only in this case the blade is too big and clunky. I also find that the soup can overflow, creating a real mess. To avoid this, try blending in batches and, again, pass through a sieve afterwards if necessary.

Sieve and muslin cloth

A large sieve is a hugely useful piece of equipment and will be called on many times throughout this book. Muslin cloth can be found online, in cookshops and in haberdashery departments. It is inexpensive and can be washed and reused if desired. A clean, dry J-cloth will also suffice.

Pestle and mortar

This is extremely useful for making pestos and pastes and will be called for in quite a few recipes. A mini food-processor will work if you don't have one.

Saucepans and baking trays

A couple of good-quality medium size saucepans and an ovenproof casserole dish will see you through almost all of the recipes in this book. I would also recommend investing in a large stockpot if you don't already have one. A couple of baking trays will come in handy for roasting vegetables too.

Ice-cube trays

Fridge and freezer space can often be scarce, so I have included instructions for making homemade stock into frozen cubes on page 16. Coconut milk is often used in small quantities throughout the book, so I would recommend opening a can and freezing tablespoon measures in an ice-cube tray to avoid waste.

Tupperware and labels

The majority of the recipes in this book are designed to serve four. If you are cooking for fewer people, the soup will keep in the fridge or freezer in most cases. Tupperware is extremely useful for storing leftover soup, and I always label containers with the name of the soup, as well as the date it was made. Empty yogurt or butter tubs, takeaway containers or even some plastic bottles are also good for storage.

Mandolin

This is a fantastic tool for thinly slicing vegetables, and extremely useful for making Vegetable Crisps (pages 45–47).

Digital weighing scales

An essential piece of equipment.

The basics

A good set of sharp knives is needed, as lots of chopping is to be done. A blunt knife is much more dangerous than a sharp one, as it can slip when chopping, so keep them sharp. A few wooden spoons, spatulas, a good-quality vegetable peeler and a ladle will also be used continually.

a few useful notes

Seasoning

I always use Maldon Sea Salt and freshly cracked black pepper. In most cases I don't give quantities; if you are unsure, add a little at first and build up until it is right for you.

Low-fat vs full-fat

I tend to eat and cook ingredients in their most natural form, so, with the exception of semi-skimmed milk, you won't find any low-fat versions here. I would happily consume less of something natural than more of something that has been processed. At least that way, I know what I'm eating!

Freezing and defrosting

Almost all of the soups here are suitable for freezing (those that are not are highlighted). I like to freeze my soup in either one- or two-person portions. If you are organised, defrost them in the fridge overnight. Otherwise, place the soup container in hot water and this will quickly defrost the soup. If you are in a rush, do this for long enough to allow you to remove the frozen soup from the container then gently reheat.

Ingredients

Using fresh ingredients is key to success, making a noticeable difference to the final flavour of your soup. Keep an eye on what you have in your fridge, and try to use ingredients before they are past the point of no return. Although soup is a great way to use things up, if a vegetable has a funky smell, this is likely to transfer to your soup.

Recipes

I cannot emphasise enough the importance of reading a recipe through, at least once, if not twice, and having everything you need ready before you start. Throughout the book there are many instructions in the ingredients lists, so placed to encourage you to do this preparation before you move on to cooking. Preparation makes for a happy and, more importantly, successful cook! Remember, recipes are but a guideline and are open to interpretation – don't be afraid to add your own twists and experiment with ideas.

Ground spices

A fantastic storecupboard addition for their long shelf life. However, nothing lasts forever and the flavour and intensity will start to deplete over time. If you haven't used a jar of ground spices in 6 months, it's time to invest in a fresh one.

Intolerances and special diets

Many of the recipes in this book are gluten- and dairy-free, vegan and vegetarian. Where they are not, it is often very simple to alter them with a few subtle changes.

Herbs

Herbs add a punchy or delicate flavour to all kinds of dishes and recipes, and my fridge is never without them. To get the most life from your herbs, wrap them in kitchen paper, dampen with cold water and refrigerate. Repeat every couple of days for a fridge life of about a week.

store-cupboard suggestions

The list below won't cover you for every recipe, but includes many that are used more than once or that are helpful to have to hand. Many of the Asian ingredients are easy to find online, so I have included those I feel are the best ones to purchase based on their shelf life and how often they are used.

Basic store-cupboard

Maldon sea salt and black peppercorns
Oil – rapeseed, olive and toasted sesame
Passata and chopped tomatoes
Pomegranate molasses
Dried wild mushrooms
Good-quality roasted red peppers (preserved in water and vinegar, not oil)
Star anise
Cinnamon sticks and ground cinnamon
Ground turmeric
Cumin (seeds and ground)
Coriander (seeds and ground)
Chilli flakes
Frozen peas
Tinned chickpeas
Black glutinous rice
Camargue and wild rice
Black quinoa
Red and yellow split lentils
Stoneground rye flour

Bicarbonate of soda
Soft-pitted prunes
Seeds – pumpkin, chia and linseeds
Walnuts
Jumbo oats

Asian

Coconut oil
Miso paste (barley and sweet miso used often)
Bonito flakes
Kombu
Black sesame seeds
Fish sauce
Soy sauce (or tamari if cooking gluten-free)
Kimchi
Tofu
Mirin
Gochujang
Edamame beans (keep in freezer)
Wonton wrappers

unusual ingredients

There are some ingredients throughout the book that may be unfamiliar. Below is a breakdown of some of the more unusual ones and where you might find them (see also Suppliers on page 156).

Black sesame seeds

White sesame seeds are easier to come by, but I favour black for their crunchier texture and more intense flavour. You can find them in health-food shops and online.

Black quinoa

This gluten-free pseudo 'grain' is a complete protein and is, in fact, a seed. You can get white, red and black quinoa, but I prefer the nuttier, sweeter taste of the black variety. You will find it in supermarkets and health-food shops. If you can't find black, use white or red.

Coconut oil

Always invest in organic virgin coconut oil for cooking. At room temperature it is solid, but quickly melts when it hits the heat.

Coconut water

This gives a delicate coconut flavour and mild sweetness to broths and stock bases. Look for unsweetened pure coconut water.

Edamame beans

Green like peas, with a more oval shape and a delicious crunchy texture, edamame are young soybeans high in protein and fibre.

They are great in soups, as a snack and in salads. You can buy them in the freezer section in supermarkets, Asian stores or online.

Gochujang

This punchy Korean chilli paste is wonderfully versatile and can be used in soups, stews, salad dressings and marinades. Once opened, store in the fridge. It can be found in Asian supermarkets or online.

Konnyaki shirataki noodles

These zero-calorie noodles hail from Japan and are a good source of dietary fibre. Alone they are almost tasteless, but they take on the flavours of whatever they are cooked with. Some big supermarkets stock these, but you are most likely to find them online.

Miso

Miso is made from fermented soybeans or grains and comes in many varieties. It has a wonderful, intense flavour and is packed with all kinds of good bacteria and antioxidants. If you have a gluten intolerance, be sure to use one that is gluten-free. Lots of supermarkets stock miso pastes now, but I always buy mine online or in Asian shops for variety and quality.

Nori

Thin sheets of dried seaweed and full of umami flavour, nori is used in this book as a garnish, almost like a seasoning. You will find it in the Asian section of your supermarket. Once opened, store in an airtight container or wrap tightly in clingfilm.

Pomegranate molasses

Found in most supermarkets, this is the concentrated juice of pomegranates. It is a powerful ingredient, intensely sweet and sour. A little goes a long way, and it can create amazing, contrasting flavours.

Soy sauce

Soy sauce is a versatile ingredient in soup-making, acting as a seasoning or a stock base and giving instant depth of flavour. Go for high-quality brands, and get to know the varieties. Some will be saltier, some more intense. Kikkoman is my favourite. If you are gluten intolerant, use tamari, but be aware that it can be stronger in flavour.

Soy, almond and hazelnut milks

Unsweetened soy and nut milks are naturally low in calories and fat. They are a great source of vitamins and minerals and boast their own unique flavour. I use them in recipes that benefit from a creamy finish. They are easy to make at home by soaking raw nuts, blending and then straining. In this book, I have used shop-bought varities for convenience. Be careful to simmer very gently once added to your soup.

Sumac

Native to the Middle East, sumac is a vibrant, coarse powder that has a lovely tangy, citrus flavour. You will find it in most supermarkets.

Tofu

Made from fresh soya milk that is curdled and then pressed into solid blocks. It is a fantastic source of protein, iron and calcium. Although it has a very delicate flavour, it acts like a sponge for the flavours it is teamed with. You will find it in supermarkets, although Asian stores often stock superior varieties and brands.

Toasted sesame oil

I use toasted rather than plain sesame oil because it has a much more intense flavour. If it is not for you, feel free to use the plain variety.

Hominy

Hominy is dried corn and is a very popular ingredient used throughout Mexican cooking. You can buy it canned and ready to use or dried. Dried hominy requires the same treatment as dried beans – overnight soaking and boiling for 2–3 hours.

Tomatillos

Tomatillos are a staple of Mexican cuisine, similar in appearance to a green tomato but with papery skins. They are sweet and sour with a crunchy texture and can be ordered online when in season. Failing this, canned tomatillos will suffice. Green tomatoes are not a suitable substitute.

homemade stock

Homemade stock — a cooking process that many of us see as an unnecessary expenditure of our time. True, indeed, when time is of the essence. There are recipes where shop bought stock or stock cubes are perfectly adequate. As this is a soup book, and as every single one of the recipes in this book will be a million times better when made using homemade stock, I am pioneering the DIY version. It takes a little organisation and planning to see through a stock recipe, but efforts are rewarded when one stock recipe gives you all you will need to create four soups each serving four people. That's a lot of soup and a lot of meals! Stock, and the majority of soups, freeze perfectly, so in the grand scheme of things you are spending time to save time. In spending that time, you are creating a meal that is infinitely more flavourful, healthy and satisfying. Convinced yet?

To make things a little easier, I have simplified the lists of ingredients. Rather than give you three separate recipes, with three separate list of ingredients, I have created one generic stock recipe that changes only depending on the bones you are using. Cooking times vary somewhat, but each process is the same. I find this easier, as it helps to learn the recipes by heart, and knowing any process by heart inevitably helps it become second nature.

As always, there are two sides to every coin, and ready made stock and stock cubes have been created for a very good reason. Time is something we often don't have to spare. There are really good stock cubes available, and many supermarkets now sell their own homemade stock. It is worth spending a little extra, if necessary, to buy quality. My favourite brands for stock cubes are Kallo — I find them the most naturally flavoured and I always keep a stash of them in my storecupboard — and Knorr stock pots, also a good option. One thing I do find misleading at times is the guideline for cube to water ratio; I've had a few unpleasantly salty soups. Start off by using half a stock cube for the full amount of water recommended on the packet and add the rest if you feel you need it.

Don't feel guilty if making stock is beyond your capabilities for whatever reason. However, I urge you to be open to it and perhaps try it a least once. If by purchasing this book you are setting off on a journey to cut back calories, or introduce more nutrition into your diet, any journey embarked on passionately from the very beginning stands a great chance of being successful!

Vegetable, Chicken and Beef Stock

After making a couple of stocks, you will find you no longer need to consult the recipe book. Furthermore, the list of ingredients is by no means set in stone, and you can use whatever you have in the fridge. However, avoid vegetables such as broccoli, cabbage, cauliflower, turnips, beetroot and potatoes.

Makes 3 litres

2 onions, peeled and roughly
    sliced
2 leeks
2 carrots
3 sticks of celery
6 sprigs of thyme
3 bay leaves
5 sprigs of parsley
10 black peppercorns
1kg raw chicken carcass (about 3)
    or 2kg beef bones, if making
    chicken or beef stock

For vegetable stock, simply cover the vegetables with 4 litres of water, bring to the boil, reduce to a simmer and cook for 40 minutes. Allow to cool for 1 hour before ladling soup through a sieve lined with muslin or a clean J-cloth. Return to the heat, bring back to the boil and reduce until you have 3 litres.

For chicken or beef stock, rinse bones under cold water and use scissors to remove any pieces of excess skin or fat.

Place bones in a large stockpot and cover with 4 litres of water. Gently bring to the boil, skimming any scum that rises to the surface (bringing the stock to the boil before adding the vegetables makes this easier. Don't be tempted to add everything all at once). Reduce to a simmer, add all of the vegetables and cook for 1½–2 hours for chicken and 4–5 hours for beef.

Let the stock cool for at least 30 minutes to allow the flavours to infuse. To strain, ladle it through a sieve lined with muslin or a clean J-cloth into a large bowl. Add a handful of ice cubes – this will encourage any fat to rise to the surface – and skim.

If any of the stocks are more than 3 litres, return to the heat and reduce. The stock will keep in the fridge for up to 1 week. Alternatively, freeze in 750ml portions or make cubes (see page 16).

A More Intensely Flavoured Stock

Roasting bones prior to cooking them in a stock creates a deeper, fuller flavour, and is often the method I prefer. Simply place the bones into a roasting tray and roast at 200°C for 45–50 minutes. When ready, drain away the fat and use some highly absorbent kitchen paper to pat off any fat still clinging to the bones. The bones are now ready to add to the stock.

Mushroom Stock

I love that this stock has only four ingredients, which all come together to give you something really powerful. Of all the stocks, it is the punchiest in flavour and the most economical too. It will replace beef stock in many of the recipes in this book, making them suitable for vegans and vegetarians. Feel free to experiment with different types of mushrooms. Dried wild mushrooms will create an even richer flavour, and you could have these on standby in your store-cupboard. This stock makes a smaller quantity than the other stocks in the book as I think it is better fresher. The recipe will give you enough stock for two soups serving four people.

Makes approx. 1½–1¾ litres
800g chestnut mushrooms, quartered
1 small onion, quartered
2 carrots, roughly chopped
2 garlic cloves, peeled

Place all of the ingredients into a stockpot with 2 litres of water. Bring to the boil, reduce to a simmer and cook for 1 hour. Strain immediately. The stock will keep in the fridge for up to 3 days and freezes well.

Homemade stock cubes

This idea came about while chatting to my Mum about my continual issue with space in my freezer. She had the brilliant idea to create frozen ice cubes of stock, rather than freezing it in batches. By reducing stock, you are condensing and concentrating its flavour dramatically, and reducing it enough to fit into an ice-cube tray will give you ready made stock cubes any time you need them. A little bit of time is required for this process, but I think it is worth it.

Makes 100ml
1 batch vegetable, chicken, beef or mushroom stock

When you have made and strained a batch of stock, return to the stockpot and boil vigorously until reduced to approximately 100ml. The beef and chicken stock will thicken and become a deep brown colour, resembling caramel in both look and consistency. Keep a close eye on it when it is almost reduced, at this stage the process speeds up significantly and the reduced stock can easily evaporate too quickly and burn. Cool and pour into four cubes of an ice-cube tray and freeze. To use, simply add one stock cube to 750ml–1 litre of water.

Japanese Dashi

Dashi is a Japanese stock that is known for its distinct umami flavour and it is used throughout Japanese cooking. Although the ingredients will most likely require some online shopping or a trip to your local Asian supermarket, this stock is easier to prepare and less expensive than many other stocks. It is as simple and straightforward as making a cup of tea. Making sure not to allow the stock to boil vigorously is about all the concentration this recipe requires. It forms the base for a traditional miso soup (see page 64) and creates a deliciously distinct and unique parsnip soup on page 44. It is made from kombu, a dried seaweed product, and bonito flakes or Katsoubushi, which comes from dried and smoked skipjack tuna. To make this stock vegan and vegetarian, simply omit the bonito flakes and add some dried shiitake mushrooms. You can make a second batch of stock by reboiling the ingredients. It will be slightly cloudier and have a stronger flavour, but it is still perfect for the purpose of the soups in this book.

Makes 2 litres
15-inch length of kombu,
  (approx. 10g)
30g shaved bonito flakes

Place the kombu with 2 litres of water in a saucepan on a very low heat. Once the liquid has just begun to simmer, after about 20–25 minutes, remove from the heat immediately and add the bonito flakes. Allow the broth to sit for a couple of minutes before straining it through a sieve lined with muslin or a clean J-cloth. Cool and refrigerate for 3–4 days or freeze until needed.

A second stock of dashi can be made with the same ingredients. Simply add 1 litre of water to the same kombu and bonito flakes and barely simmer for 15–20 minutes. Add 10g fresh bonito flakes to the stock and allow to stand for a couple of minutes before straining, as you have done above.

Turmeric and Lemongrass Paste

Making powerfully flavoured pastes makes it very easy to create a wonderful broth without the time it takes to make stock. This paste is inspired by the flavours I experienced while travelling around Cambodia and Vietnam. A small hand-held blender will do all the work for you when creating this paste — it couldn't be easier!

Makes roughly 260g
(calories per tablespoon)

 calories 16 DF GF

Carbs 0.8g   Sugar 0.5g   Protein 0.4g   Fibre 0.5g   Fat 1.1g   Sat Fat 0.9g   Salt trace

2 fresh red bird's eye chillies
4 cloves of garlic, peeled
4 sticks of lemongrass, roughly chopped
30g ginger, roughly sliced
4 pink Asian shallots or 2 standard shallots
2½ teaspoons turmeric powder
50g fresh coconut (can be found ready-prepared in supermarkets)
1 teaspoon shrimp paste

Place all of the ingredients in a mini hand-held blender with 4–5 tablespoons of water and blend to a paste. It will be reluctant to break down at first, but blend for a couple of minutes and you will get there!

Walnut Miso Paste

I first came across this in a little noodle bar called Koya in Soho, London. I was blown away by its addictive mellow flavour and wanted to recreate something similar here. It transforms the parsnip soup on page 44, and it adds a fantastic depth of flavour to the lunch noodle pots on pages 81–84. Store in your fridge and use to dress steamed vegetables or as a base for a salad dressing.

Makes roughly 100g
(calories per tablespoon)

calories 15 DF V VE

Carbs 1.3g   Sugar 0.4g   Protein 0.5g   Fibre 0g   Fat 0.8g   Sat Fat 0.1g   Salt 0.3g

20g walnuts, roughly chopped (somewhere between chunky and fine)
35g sweet white miso
15g barley miso
1 tablespoon mirin
1 tablespoon tamari or light soy sauce

Toast the walnuts in a dry frying pan over a medium heat until golden brown. Chopping them first is important to increase the surface area you are toasting — this flavour is an integral part of the paste.

Mix the misos with the mirin and tamari or soy sauce. Add the toasted walnuts and mix thoroughly.

smooth soups

A smooth soup — a variety of ingredients cooked in stock and blended until silky smooth — is based on the simplest of concepts. However, this simplicity opens up a whole world of possibilities. There are infinite combinations you can play with by mixing and matching all kinds of vegetables and, at times, fruits, for a quirky layer of flavour. Spices, herbs and garnishes can all serve to transform a simple idea into a remarkable dish.

I love to play with flavours, and a smooth soup is one of the most interesting ways to do this. There is a purity about a blended soup — a spoonful uninterrupted by texture that allows you to really appreciate and savour the qualities and characteristics of your chosen ingredients.

There are many classic combinations out there, all very well documented, so I have taken the soups in this chapter down a somewhat unexpected route. You will find that burning something is not always such a bad thing with the Blackened Tomato and Ancho Chilli Soup, and that using a garnish of chilled zingy grapes enhances the richness of a Thyme and Mustard Roasted Jerusalem Artichoke Soup by cutting right through it. The sweet potato soup is anything but predictable flavoured with sumac and pomegranate and piled high with crunchy nuts, coriander and pomegranate seeds.

These soups are very much a product of my imagination, and their difference makes them all the more delicious. They are fun and designed to get you excited about what you could be eating today!

blackened tomato and ancho chilli with citrus soured cream

This recipe transforms a few humble tomatoes into a charred, smoky, sweet, rich and deeply satisfying soup with a subtle hint of warmth from dried chillies. You will be asked to go against one of your main instincts in the kitchen and deliberately burn something. Crazy, I know — but it works!

Serves 4   (DF and VE if not using soured cream)

calories 85

Carbs 12.5g   Sugar 12.5g   Protein 2.5g   Fibre 4g   Fat 2g   Sat Fat 1g   Salt trace

1.7kg medium tomatoes on the vine
2–3 dried Ancho chillies
30g soured cream
juice and zest of 1 lime
salt and pepper

Preheat the grill to its highest temperature. Slice each tomato in half and arrange cut side up on a baking tray. Place the tray on a shelf as close to the grill as possible and cook for 30–40 minutes until nicely blackened.

Meanwhile, place the dried chillies in a bowl with the tomato vines, and cover with 500ml boiling water. Set aside. Mix the lime zest with the soured cream and season with salt and pepper. Refrigerate until needed.

When the tomatoes are ready, carefully turn them over and grill for a further 5 minutes, or until the skins are crisp and charred. This may happen quickly so keep a watchful eye.

When ready, discard the vines and transfer the tomatoes and all of their juices into a blender, along with the chillies, their soaking water and lime juice. Blend until smooth, season to taste, reheat and serve garnished with a spoonful of citrus soured cream.

Tip: Store leftover dried chillies in an airtight jar. They will keep indefinitely.

golden beetroot, fennel and saffron with poached rainbow trout

This is a meal in a bowl — extremely substantial and filling. You can play around with the fish you use. Some chargrilled scallops would be delicious, with a little flourish of finely chopped chorizo. If you have any left over, it is lovely to serve the fish cold on top of the reheated soup. The contrast of hot and cold works brilliantly.

Serves 4

Carbs 9g   Sugar 8g   Protein 13g   Fibre 5g   Fat 4.5g   Sat Fat 0.8g   Salt 0.3g

800ml vegetable stock
1–2 fillets of rainbow trout
   (approx. 200g), skin left on
½ tablespoon olive oil
1 small leek, sliced
1 garlic clove, chopped
2 sprigs of thyme, leaves picked
1 large fennel bulb,
   approximately 250–300g,
   roughly chopped (set aside tips
   for garnish)
400g golden beetroot, peeled
   and grated
generous pinch of saffron
salt and pepper
dill, to garnish
1 lemon, cut into wedges

Bring the stock to the boil in a saucepan or frying pan deep enough to fit the fish. When simmering, place the fish in the liquid and cook gently for 5 minutes. When ready, remove the fish to a plate or dish. Cover with tinfoil and a tea-towel to keep warm. Skim any froth, oils or fat that have risen to the surface of the stock.

Meanwhile, heat the oil with 1 tablespoon of water in a medium saucepan and sauté the leek, garlic and thyme for 5 minutes. Add the fennel, beetroot, saffron and reserved stock and bring to the boil. Reduce to a simmer and cook for 20 minutes.

Blend until smooth, then return to the saucepan and keep on a very low heat. Use a sharp-pointed knife to peel the skin from the fish, and gently flake the flesh, being careful to leave behind any bones.

Pour the soup into heated bowls, and top with the warm flaked rainbow trout. Garnish with dill and the fennel tips and serve immediately with a wedge of lemon.

miso roasted butternut squash

This soup boasts an amazing depth of flavour thanks to the addition of some beautifully intense barley miso paste. You can play around with other types of miso here too. The nutritious properties of the paste deplete when cooked, so some is kept back and added when blending.

Serves 4   (GF if using GF miso)

Carbs 20g Sugar 9g Protein 4g Fibre 4.8g Fat 3.5g Sat Fat 2.5g Salt 0.9g

1 large butternut squash
(approx. 1kg)
2½ tablespoons barley miso
1 tablespoon coconut oil, melted
if solid
3 slices of ginger plus 15g peeled
and finely grated
2 garlic cloves, peeled
1 red chilli
1 lime, cut into 4 wedges

Preheat the oven to 180°C/gas mark 4.

Peel and halve the butternut squash, discarding the seeds, and roughly chop into 2cm cubes. Place in a deep roasting tin. In a small bowl, mix together 1 tablespoon of barley miso with the melted coconut oil. Pour all over the squash, mixing well. Roast for 35–40 minutes, turning halfway through to ensure an even roast.

Meanwhile, prepare the stock. Place the slices of ginger, the garlic and red chilli in a saucepan with 850ml water. Bring to the boil and simmer with the lid on for 15 minutes. Remove from the heat and allow the flavours to infuse.

When the squash is ready, remove the aromatics from the stock and transfer to a blender with the roasted squash, remaining miso paste and grated ginger. Blend until very smooth and season to taste.

Serve with the lime wedges and Crispy Sesame Tofu Fingers (page 28).

crispy sesame tofu fingers

These are great served with the Miso-roasted Butternut Squash soup on page 26. They also make an excellent snack, served with some chilli sauce, such as Sriracha, or can be used as a garnish or crispy addition to a salad. Simply make them as cubes rather than long fingers.

Serves 4

calories 68   DF   V

Carbs 2.6g   Sugar 0.2g   Protein 6g   Fibre 0.1g   Fat 3.7g   Sat Fat 0.6g   Salt 0.4g

200g firm tofu
2 tablespoons tamari or soy sauce
10g ginger, finely grated
1 free-range egg white, lightly whisked
10g panko breadcrumbs
5g black sesame seeds
¼ teaspoon chilli powder
generous pinch of salt and pepper

Drain the tofu and pat dry with some kitchen paper. Squeeze as much liquid from the tofu as possible without breaking it up. Slice into four fingers and marinate in the tamari or soy sauce and ginger for a minimum of 30 minutes or overnight if possible.

Preheat the oven to 240°C/gas mark 9. Remove the tofu from the marinade and brush off any clumps of ginger. Place between two pieces of kitchen paper and apply some gentle pressure to squeeze out any excess liquid.

Combine the breadcrumbs, black sesame seeds, chilli powder, salt and pepper. Dip the tofu pieces into the egg white and then into the breadcrumb mixture, making sure they are evenly coated.

Place on a baking tray lined with parchment and bake for 5 minutes, turning halway through, until nicely browned and crispy. Serve immediately alongside Miso-roasted Butternut Squash Soup, see page 26.

thyme and mustard-roasted Jerusalem artichoke and garlic with red grapes

These nobbly vegetables are diamonds in the rough. They are next to impossible to peel, so I simply don't bother. There's a lot of flavour and goodness in the skin, so why waste time discarding it? Garlic becomes a sweeter, creamier, more subdued version of itself when roasted, so don't be alarmed by the quantity used here. And chilled red grapes provide some sharp sweetness, which cuts through the caramel tones of the roasted vegetables beautifully.

Serves 4

Carbs 27g   Sugar 6.5g   Protein 5g   Fibre 11g   Fat 2.5g   Sat Fat 0.3g   Salt 0.8g

900g Jerusalem artichokes, thoroughly washed and halved
½ head of garlic
5–6 sprigs of thyme, leaves picked, plus extra to serve
½ tablespoon olive oil
¾ tablespoon English or Dijon mustard
juice of ½ lemon
salt and pepper
750ml vegetable or chicken stock
small handful of chilled red grapes, quartered

Preheat the oven to 180°C/gas mark 4. Place the prepared artichokes on a baking tray with the garlic and sprinkle the thyme all over.

Mix the olive oil, mustard and lemon juice in a small bowl and drizzle all over the vegetables, then using your hands, make sure they are thoroughly coated. Season generously with salt and pepper and roast. The cooking time will vary slightly depending on what size Jerusalem artichokes you are using. Give them at least 30 minutes. If they are still firm after this time, cook until soft.

Bring the chicken stock to the boil. Now transfer, with the roasted vegetables, to a blender and blitz until very smooth. Serve topped with the chilled red grapes and fresh thyme leaves.

chilled cucumber, almond and lemon

This soup is light, refreshing, zingy, rehydrating and, most importantly, wonderfully cooling. You could chill the soup using plain ice cubes, but some decorative pomegranate ice cubes will add to the overall beauty of the dish, while adding some texture too.

Serves 4 GF DF V VE

Carbs 4.3g   Sugar 4.2g   Protein 1.4g   Fibre 1.1g   Fat 1g   Sat Fat 0.1g   Salt 0.1g

550g cucumber (about
1½ cucumbers), roughly
chopped
300ml unsweetened fresh
almond milk (not UHT)
zest and juice of 1 lemon
2–3 sprigs of basil, leaves picked
(about 10 leaves)
2–3 sprigs of mint, leaves picked
(about 10 leaves)
a handful of pomegranate seeds
(optional)
finely sliced cucumber (optional)

Blend all ingredients together until very smooth. Chill for up to two hours or overnight if possible. Serve in glasses.

To make the ice cubes, simply place some pomegranate seeds, along with some finely sliced cucumber into an ice-cube tray, cover with water and freeze. I use small Lebanese cucumbers here, but you can use whatever is available.

Note: some edible flowers also look beautiful when frozen in ice-cube trays.

pumpkin seed and prune rye soda bread

Soda bread is the Holy Grail of bread making — no kneading or proving required. Dry ingredients are gently mixed with wet ingredients before being baked — it couldn't be more straightforward! Rich and full of goodness, this loaf should be thinly sliced. It's a good idea to freeze some slices to have to hand when you need them. You can also use it to make croutons, crackers and savoury breadcrumbs to serve as a garnish or side for lots of the soups in this book.

Makes 35 slices   calories 48   V

. . . .

Carbs 6.3g   Sugar 1.1g   Protein 1.5g   Fibre 1.3g   Fat 1.5g   Sat Fat 0.2g   Salt 0.2g

. . . .

70g soft pitted prunes (about 6 small prunes)
185g stoneground rye flour
50g strong white bread flour
I teaspoon bicarbonate of soda
I teaspoon sea salt
100g pumpkin seeds
200ml buttermilk
I tablespoon oats

450g loaf tin, greased and lined

Preheat the oven to 180°C/gas mark 4. Soak the prunes in 80ml of boiling hot water.

Place the flours, bicarbonate of soda, sea salt and 80g of the pumpkin seeds in a medium bowl and mix well. Add the buttermilk to the prunes and soaking liquid and blitz to a smooth purée. Pour into the dry ingredients, mixing very gently until you have a wet and sticky dough. Don't over-mix as this will result in a tough bread.

Transfer the dough to the prepared loaf tin, sprinkle with the remaining pumpkin seeds and the oats, and flatten down slightly. Bake for 40 minutes, turning upside down in the tin for the last 10 minutes of baking to get a nice even crust. Transfer to a wire rack to cool.

ideas for leftover soda bread

Soda bread crackers

These are so easy to make and provide a lovely bit of crunch and texture when eaten alongside soup. It is important to slice the bread as thinly as possible, so best to make when the loaf is a few days old. Delicious topped with avocado and tomato, a little scrambled egg or a finely chopped salsa of tomato, spring onion, cucumber, avocado and sweetcorn. Use with recipes such as the Aromatic Dhal soup (page 122).

Serves 4

Carbs 11g   Sugar 0.4g   Protein 1.6g   Fibre 0.5g   Fat 0.3g   Sat Fat 0.1g   Salt 0.1g

8 very thin slices of soda bread (to serve 4)

Preheat the oven to 200°C/gas mark 6. Lay the slices on a baking tray and cook for 8–10 minutes, turning halfway through and keeping a close eye to ensure they are not burning. You can make a batch of these and store in an airtight container. They will keep for about a week.

Croutons

Croutons are a great garnish for soups, and this soda bread version is delicious. For a bit of extra flavour, you could rub each slice with a clove of garlic before cutting.

Serves 4

Carbs 7g   Sugar 1.2g   Protein 1.8g   Fibre 1.3g   Fat 1.6g   Sat Fat 0.3g   Salt trace

3 slices soda bread, each cut into 8
½ tablespoon rapeseed oil or olive oil
salt and pepper

Preheat the oven to 180°C/gas mark 4. Dress the croutons with the oil, salt and pepper and transfer to a baking tray. Bake for 10–12 minutes, checking and turning a couple of times while cooking. They will keep for 2–3 days in an airtight container.

Savoury breadcrumbs

This is a great way to add texture, substance and another layer of flavour to lots of soups. The breadcrumbs cook extremely quickly so keep a close eye on them. Once cooked, I like to add herbs such as thyme, tarragon, oregano or rosemary. Chilli powder is nice too, as is ground ginger or smoked paprika. A half teaspoon of miso stirred through the breadcrumbs before cooking is also delicious.

Serves 4

Carbs 8g   Sugar 0.3g   Protein 1.2g   Fibre 0.4g   Fat 0.2g   Sat Fat 0.1g   Salt 0.1g

3 slices bread, blitzed into breadcrumbs
salt and pepper

Preheat the oven to 200°C/gas mark 6. Blitz three slices of bread into breadcrumbs, spread in a thin layer on a baking tray and season with salt and pepper. Cook for no more than 3 minutes, checking a few times to prevent burning. The breadcrumbs will continue to crisp as they cool. They will keep for 2–3 days in an airtight container.

sichuan-roasted red pepper with five-spice edamame relish

Sichuan peppercorns are native to the Sichuan province of China, but are not actually peppercorns. They are the dried berries of a type of ash tree and have a lemony and peppery fragrance. Beautifully aromatic, they leave an amazing numbing or tingling sensation on the palate, making this soup feel as though it has a cooling rather than warming effect.

Serves 4 calories 125 DF V VE (GF if using tamari)

Carbs 16g   Sugar 16g   Protein 5.5g   Fibre 8g   Fat 2g   Sat Fat 0.3g   Salt 2g

1 tablespoon Sichuan peppercorns
2 garlic cloves, peeled
pinch of salt
3 tablespoons tamari or dark soy sauce
1kg red peppers, each deseeded and cut into 8 (set aside ½ a pepper for Five-spice Edamame Relish, below)
250g tomatoes, quartered
1 medium red onion, peeled and roughly sliced
650ml vegetable or chicken stock

For the Five-spice Edamame Relish (30 calories per serving; not suitable for freezing)
70g frozen edamame beans
½ red pepper (see above), diced
⅛ teaspoon five-spice powder
juice of ½ a lime
pinch of salt

Preheat the oven to 200°C/gas mark 6. Toast the Sichuan peppercorns in a dry frying pan for 2 minutes. Grind in a pestle and mortar, along with the garlic and salt, to a rough paste. Add the tamari or soy sauce and mix well.

Place the peppers and tomatoes in a large bowl, along with the sliced onion, and pour over the Sichuan peppercorn mixture. Use your hands to thoroughly mix, ensuring all the vegetables are coated.

Divide between two baking trays and roast for 40 minutes, turning occasionally. When ready, transfer to a large bowl, cover with clingfilm and leave to stand for 10 minutes.

Simmer the edamame beans for 5 minutes, refresh under cold water and pat dry. Mix with the red pepper, five-spice powder, lime juice and salt. Refrigerate until needed.

Heat the stock and, when almost boiling, pour three quarters of it into a blender and add the vegetables. Blend until silky smooth and add enough stock to achieve your desired consistency. Return to the saucepan and bring back to the boil before serving with the edamame relish.

Note: if using a stick blender for this soup, you may need to pass it through a sieve for a very smooth consistency.

sweetcorn, lemongrass and turmeric

This is remarkably decadent considering nothing creamy is added, which would often be the case with a sweetcorn soup. A fantastic filling lunch, or serve in small portions as a starter to a more formal meal.

Serves 4

Carbs 11.5g   Sugar 3.5g   Protein 5g   Fibre 3.7g   Fat 4.5g   Sat Fat 2g   Salt trace

I medium leek, trimmed, halved
   and roughly chopped
¾ tablespoon coconut oil,
   melted if solid
50g Turmeric and Lemongrass
   Paste (page 18)
550g sweetcorn, freshly removed
   from 4–5 cobs
fresh coriander, to garnish

Sauté the leek in ½ tablespoon coconut oil and I tablespoon water until softened, about 5–7 minutes, stirring occasionally. Stir in the paste, and cook for a couple of minutes. Add all but 100g of the sweetcorn along with 900ml water and the cobs for added flavour. Bring to the boil, reduce to a simmer and cook for 15 minutes.

Turn on your grill to high. Place the reserved corn along with the remaining ¼ tablespoon of coconut oil onto a baking tray, mix together and place under the grill for 5–8 minutes. When starting to char remove, season and set aside.

When the soup is ready, leave to cool a little before removing the cobs, then blend until smooth. Pass through a sieve to achieve a silky smooth soup, season to taste and serve garnished with the charred sweetcorn and some fresh coriander.

celeriac with horseradish, lemon and parsley

This combination of flavours is one of my all time favourites and I never enjoy it more than when it is presented in a lusciously smooth bowl of soup. Enjoy with a few slices of Pumpkin Seed and Prune Soda Bread (page 32).

Serves 4 calories 144 GF V

Carbs 17g   Sugar 7g   Protein 6g   Fibre 10g   Fat 3.5g   Sat Fat 1g   Salt 0.5g

1 small leek, trimmed, cleaned and roughly sliced

1 garlic clove, roughly chopped

1 medium potato, peeled and diced

½ tablespoon olive oil

1 small celeriac, roughly 600g, peeled and roughly chopped into 1cm cubes

2 peeled strips of lemon rind

750ml vegetable stock

20g parsley, stalks reserved and leaves roughly chopped

1 bay leaf

2 tablespoons freshly grated horseradish (use from a jar if you can't find fresh)

1 teaspoon Dijon mustard

250ml semi-skimmed milk

juice of 1 lemon

In a saucepan, sauté the leek, garlic and potato in the olive oil and 1 tablespoon of water on a medium heat for 5 minutes, stirring frequently. Add a splash more water if the vegetables stick to the pan.

Add the celeriac, lemon rind and stock. Tie the reserved parsley stalks and bay leaf together with a piece of string and add to the soup. Bring to a gentle simmer, and cook with the lid on for 30 minutes.

Five minutes before the soup is finished, remove the herbs and lemon rind. Stir in the grated horseradish, mustard and milk. Simmer for the remaining 5 minutes, and then blend, adding a splash of water or stock if the soup is too thick for you. Season with salt and pepper. Stir the lemon juice and chopped parsley through the soup immediately before serving.

sweet potato, sumac and pomegranate with roasted peanuts, coriander and lime

Sometimes I find sweet potato soup a little too sweet, but not here — teamed with citrusy sumac, sour pomegranate, aromatic coriander and crunchy roasted peanuts, it is what a bowl of fun should look like!

Serves 4 calories 213 DF GF (V/VE if using vegetable stock)

Carbs 32g Sugar 16g Protein 5g Fibre 6g Fat 6g Sat Fat 2g Salt 0.2g

I medium onion, roughly
  chopped
2 garlic cloves, roughly chopped
I red chilli, deseeded and
  roughly chopped
I teaspoon sumac
½ tablespoon coconut oil
400g sweet potatoes, peeled and
  roughly chopped into 2cm
  cubes
3–4 vine tomatoes (approx.
  300g), roughly chopped
850ml chicken or vegetable stock
I½ tablespoons pomegranate
  molasses

Garnish
small bunch of fresh coriander
  leaves
30g roasted salted peanuts,
  roughly chopped
seeds from ½ pomegranate
a few pinches of sumac
I lime, cut into 4 wedges

Sauté the onion, garlic, chilli and sumac in the coconut oil and I tablespoon of water until soft and translucent — about 5 minutes.

Add the sweet potatoes, tomatoes and stock, bring to the boil and then simmer with the lid on for about 20 minutes, until the potatoes are tender. Leave to cool a little before adding the pomegranate molasses. Blend until silky smooth and season.

Garnish with the coriander, chopped peanuts, pomegranate seeds, sumac and wedge of lime.

Tip: if you have a gluten intolerance and wish to use shop-bought peanuts check they are gluten-free.

parsnip and walnut miso soup

Parsnips and the Walnut Miso Paste make a beautiful pairing. Homemade dashi is what really makes this soup unique and is worth the little extra effort to achieve the resulting flavour. Served with Sriracha Parsnip Crisps (opposite) this soup makes for a sweet, spicy bowl of joy.

Serves 4

Carbs 23g   Sugar 10g   Protein 4g   Fibre 7.5g   Fat 5g   Sat Fat 0.6g   Salt 1g

1 garlic clove, finely chopped
1 banana shallot, chopped
15g ginger, roughly chopped
½ tablespoon toasted sesame oil
600g parsnips, peeled and cut
  into 2cm cubes
750ml Japanese Dashi, (page 17)
40g Walnut Miso Paste (page 18)

Sauté the garlic, shallot and ginger in the toasted sesame oil and 1 tablespoon of water for about 5 minutes until soft and translucent. Add the parsnips and dashi, bring to the boil and simmer gently with the lid on for 25–30 minutes, until the parsnips are tender.

Transfer to a blender and blitz until silky smooth. Stir in the Walnut Miso Paste; alternatively, swirl a spoonful of the paste into the soup before serving. Garnish with Sriracha Parsnip Crisps.

vegetable crisps

Vegetable crisps couldn't be easier to make and are a delicious garnish
for lots of soups. They also make a great healthy snack. They are best eaten
on the day they are cooked, as they won't keep in an airtight container.
A mandolin will make your life so much easier here.

Sriracha Parsnip Crisps

Serves 4 as a garnish
(calories per crisp)

calories 3   DF   GF   V   VE

Carbs 0.5g   Sugar 0.2g   Protein 0.1g   Fibre 0.2g   Fat 0.0g   Sat Fat 0.0g   Salt trace

1 large parsnip, washed and
   peeled
1 tablespoon Sriracha
salt and pepper

Preheat the oven to 150°C/gas mark 2. Thinly slice the
parsnip into circles, about 2mm thick, or use a potato
peeler to create long, thin strips. Coat with the Sriracha,
salt and pepper and lay flat on a baking tray lined with
baking parchment. These crisps can take minutes to cook,
depending on the size of the parsnips. Give them 5 minutes,
and check regularly, removing any that are cooking
quicker. Bigger ones may require a minute or so longer.

Beetroot Crisps

Serves 4 as a garnish
(calories per crisp)

calories 3   DF   GF   V   VE

Carbs 0.1g   Sugar 0.1g   Protein trace   Fibre trace   Fat 0.2g   Sat Fat 0.0g   Salt trace

1 beetroot, washed and peeled
   (you could also try a mix of
   red, pink and golden)
1 tablespoon rapeseed or olive oil
salt and pepper
flavour ideas: ground fennel
   seeds, sumac and fresh thyme

Preheat the oven to 150°C/gas mark 2. Thinly slice
the beetroot into perfect circles about 2mm thick.
Thoroughly coat with the oil, salt and pepper and any
other flavour you have chosen. Lay on a baking tray lined
with parchment and bake for 15 minutes, turning over
halfway through cooking. You may need to do this in
batches or use two baking trays. Check every 5 minutes,
and remove any that are already cooked — smaller circles
will cook quicker. Leave to cool before serving.

Peppered Sweet Potato Crisps

Serves 4 as a garnish
(calories per crisp)

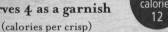 calories 12 DF GF V VE

Carbs 1.7g   Sugar 0.5g   Protein 0.1g   Fibre 0.3g   Fat 0.5g   Sat Fat 0.0g   Salt 0.1g

½ sweet potato, washed and
   peeled
1 tablespoon rapeseed oil
½ teaspoon freshly ground
   pepper (a mix of black, pink
   and white peppercorns would
   be nice, too)
generous pinch of salt

Preheat the oven to 150°C/gas mark 2. Thinly slice the
sweet potato into circles. Alternatively, you could use a
potato peeler to create long, thin strips. Coat with the oil,
pepper and salt and lay on a lined baking tray. You may
need to do this in batches, or use two baking trays. Bake
for 12 minutes, checking regularly and removing any that
are cooking faster. Leave to cool before serving.

broths and consommés

My love affair with broths began when I was travelling in South East Asia. Every day for breakfast, lunch or dinner we would have a bowl of hot broth brimming with silky noodles, fresh vegetables and herbs. No two were ever the same and not one failed to blow me away. It sparked a profound passion and respect for the wonder that is a bowl of broth — a perfectly balanced blend of flavours, effortlessly healthy and wonderfully wholesome.

It can be as simple as a miso soup, adorned with nothing more than tofu, spring onions and wakame, or as complex as the Hoi An New Wives' Broth, which is a celebration of harmonious yet dynamic flavours. Some, such as Wonton Soup, are well known favourites, whereas others, such as the Korean Steak Tartare in Broth, are my own adaptation of a traditional dish. An intensely flavoured Turmeric and Lemongrass paste is a quick fire way to add bold flavour to a broth without needing much time. The laborious aspect of a consommé is overcome by applying the same technique to fruit and vegetables, providing recipes that are a lot less time-consuming, but incredibly flavoursome. The essence of tomatoes is captured in the Tomato Consommé Cooler, boasting flavour so invigorating, it will awaken each and every taste bud.

Broths are, at times, somewhat demanding of either time or effort. However, the satisfaction to be gained from stepping off the treadmill to spend a little uninterrupted time in the kitchen will make it all worthwhile. These are recipes worth shutting out the world for!

sea bream, coconut and lime broth

While in Cambodia I ate the most unusual crab and lime soup – like nothing I had ever tasted, its vibrancy and clarity snapped my senses awake. This recipe is a nod to that memory.

Serves 4 calories 216 DF GF

Carbs 16.8g   Sugar 14.5g   Protein 25.3g   Fibre 3g   Fat 4.5g   Sat Fat 0.4g   Salt 2.8g

650ml coconut water
3 stalks of lemongrass, bruised and cut into 2cm lengths
5 kaffir lime leaves
4 garlic cloves, peeled
8 Asian shallots, peeled and quartered
20g ginger, peeled and sliced
2 tablespoons fish sauce
1 whole sea bream (approx. 500–600g), gutted and cleaned
4 red bird's eye chillis, 1 halved, others finely sliced
15g each of Thai basil, mint and coriander, leaves picked
3 spring onions, thinly sliced
240g beansprouts
juice of 3 limes

Mango relish
½ mango, peeled and finely sliced or shredded
1 red bird's eye chilli, finely chopped
½ tablespoon fish sauce
½ teaspoon black pepper

Place all of the ingredients up to and including the sea bream, and the halved bird's eye chilli, with 1 litre of water in a deep heavy-based saucepan wide enough to hold the fish lying flat. Bring to a simmer and cook for 15 minutes.

Meanwhile, make the mango relish. Combine all ingredients, mix well and taste for seasoning.

Divide the 3 finely sliced bird's eye chillies between 4 bowls, along with the herbs, spring onions and beansprouts.

When cooked, remove the fish from the broth, peel away the skin and carefully remove the white flesh from the bones. Divide between the bowls.

Stir the lime juice through the broth, tasting for seasoning. If you feel it requires further seasoning, add a dash of fish sauce. Strain and pour over the ingredients in each bowl. Garnish with the mango relish and serve immediately.

Note: kaffir lime leaves can be found in Asian supermarkets, often in the freezer section. Waitrose now sells fresh kaffir lime leaves, but if you can't find any fresh or frozen, most big supermarkets stock dried leaves.

Not suitable for freezing

green vegetable broth with pistou chicken skewers

This soup is a gorgeous contrast of crunchy refreshing vegetables and deliciously charred chicken skewers. Get them on the barbecue if you have one going!

Serves 2

Carbs 13g   Sugar 7g   Protein 37g   Fibre 5g   Fat 10g   Sat Fat 1.5g   Salt 0.3g

For the pistou

2 garlic cloves, peeled

50g basil, roughly chopped

1 tablespoon olive oil

1 medium ripe tomato, roughly chopped

For the skewers and broth

2 small chicken breasts, roughly 250g

75ml buttermilk

wooden skewers, soaked in cold water

1 banana shallot, finely diced

2 garlic cloves, finely chopped

3 sun-dried tomatoes, roughly chopped

½ tablespoon olive oil

1 tablespoon tomato purée

1 litre vegetable stock

150g baby courgettes, sliced

75g asparagus, diced

75g French beans, trimmed and cut into 1cm lengths

75g sugar-snap peas, cut into 3

First make the pistou. Pound the garlic with a pinch of salt in a pestle and mortar until smooth. Add the basil and grind until almost smooth. Add the olive oil, then the tomato and pound everything to a rough paste (or use a mini hand-held blender for this). Season to taste.

Place the chicken breasts between 2 pieces of clingfilm and, using a rolling pin, bash until they are nice and thin. When ready, slice each breast into 4 strips lengthwise. Mix half of the pistou with the buttermilk, add the chicken and marinate for a minimum of 30 minutes, or overnight if possible. When ready, thread the chicken onto the soaked skewers and set aside.

In a medium saucepan, sauté the shallot, garlic and sun-dried tomato in the oil and 1 tablespoon of water until softened. Add the tomato purée and stock, bring to the boil and simmer for 10 minutes.

Meanwhile, place a griddle pan over a high heat and cook the chicken skewers for 3–4 minutes on each side.

Add the vegetables to the broth and simmer for 3–4 minutes. Season to taste. Serve with the skewers sitting along the rim of the bowl and the remaining pistou to stir through.

Broth only suitable for freezing

korean steak tartare (yukhoe) in broth

Yukhoe is a Korean steak tartare dish, traditionally served with Asian pear, egg yolk and pine nuts. Here it sits within a punchy, spicy broth, flavoured with gochujang, a Korean chilli paste. This is an intensely flavoured soup and epitomises using the very best ingredients and treating them in quite a simple way.

Serves 4 calories 122 DF (GF if using tamari)

Carbs 6g   Sugar 6g   Protein 12.5g   Fibre 1.1g   Fat 5g   Sat Fat 1.7g   Salt 2.8g

200g best-quality fillet steak
1 garlic clove, peeled
20g ginger, peeled and finely chopped or grated
3 tablespoons tamari or light soy sauce
1 teaspoon toasted sesame oil
1 teaspoon honey
3 teaspoons Korean chilli powder (if using plain chilli powder ½ teaspoon is sufficient)
1 spring onion, finely chopped
750ml mushroom stock (page 16)
2 teaspoons gochujang
2 teaspoons mirin (optional)
5g parsley, finely chopped
1½ teaspoons black or white sesame seeds, toasted

Slice the beef into very thin strips, then cut into tiny dice. It is very important to chop the beef as finely as possible. Pound the garlic and ginger in a pestle and mortar to a smooth paste and add two tablespoons of the tamari or soy sauce, the sesame oil, honey and chilli powder. (If you don't have a pestle and mortar, chop the garlic and ginger together until they resemble a paste.) Thoroughly mix the resulting sauce with the beef, along with the spring onion, and chill in the fridge until needed.

Gently heat the mushroom stock until just boiling, then reduce the heat to keep it at a simmer. Add the gochujang, remaining tamari or soy sauce and mirin, if using, and whisk to dissolve the chilli paste. Taste and adjust to your liking if necessary.

Just before serving, add half of the parsley to the tartare and mix well. Neatly divide the mixture between 4 bowls, and pour in the broth. Top the tartare with the remaining parsley and the sesame seeds. Serve immediately.

Note: the broth base can be made ahead and frozen, but the tartare must be made fresh. Korean chilli powder and gochujang can be found in Asian supermarkets.

wonton soup

You are most likely to find wonton wrappers online or in Asian supermarkets. Buy a few packets, and pop what you don't use in the freezer. Divide and freeze in batches based on the number called for in a particular recipe (I find 12–16 is a good quantity, or 8 in the case of the recipe for wonton crisps — see page 58).

Serves 4

Carbs 17g   Sugar 1.7g   Protein 18g   Fibre 1.6g   Fat 6g   Sat Fat 1.6g   Salt 1.5g

150g raw prawns, deveined and finely chopped
150g minced pork
8 dried Chinese mushrooms, rehydrated and finely chopped
28g chives, finely chopped
1½ teaspoons sesame oil
2 teaspoons tamari or light soy sauce
2 teaspoons shaoxing wine
1 teaspoon oyster sauce
pinch of salt
12 wonton wrappers
1.2 litres vegetable stock
generous pinch of white pepper
4 baby pak choi, quartered

In a bowl, mix together the prawns, pork, mushrooms, chives, 1 teaspoon each of the sesame oil, tamari or soy sauce and shaoxing wine, the oyster sauce and salt.

Working with one wonton wrapper at a time, keeping the rest covered with a damp tea-towel so that they don't dry out, lay the wrapper in front of you, so that it is in the shape of a diamond. Place a tablespoon of the mixture in the middle and, using your finger, moisten the edges of the wrapper with a little water. Fold the wrapper in half so that it is the shape of a triangle and press the edges together to seal. Now bring the two bottom corners together, dampen the edges again and seal. It should resemble tortellini.

Fill a large saucepan with water and bring to a gentle simmer. Cook the wontons in batches, for 5 minutes at a time, turning over halfway through cooking. It is important not to vigorously boil the water otherwise the wontons will fall apart.

Meanwhile, in a separate pan, bring the stock to a boil and season with the remaining sesame oil, tamari or soy sauce, shaoxing rice wine and white pepper. Add the pak choi and cook for a couple of minutes.

Divide the wontons between 4 bowls, along with the pak choi, then pour in the stock and serve immediately.

Tips: If you can't find dried Chinese mushrooms, use dried shiitake or porcini mushrooms, which can be found in most big supermarkets.

You can make the wontons ahead and freeze them uncooked. Simply place on some parchment paper in a Tupperware box, cover with a tight-fitting lid and freeze. Cook them from frozen, adding 2–3 minutes to the cooking time.

hoisin sesame seed wonton crisps

Wonton wrappers can be kept in batches in the freezer ready to make these crisps at the drop of a hat. They are a quick and easy side to throw together for a soup and are a delicious snack all on their own. They will keep for a couple of days in an airtight container.

Serves 4 calories 81 (VE if using vegetarian hoisin sauce)

Carbs 9g   Sugar 0.7g   Protein 2.8g   Fibre 0.6g   Fat 3.5g   Sat Fat 0.6g   Salt 0.2g

8 wonton wrappers
1 tablespoon hoisin sauce
1½ tablespoons sesame seeds,
   white or black or a mixture
salt and pepper

Preheat the oven to 180°C/gas mark 4 and line a baking tray with parchment paper. Brush both sides of each wonton wrapper with the hoisin sauce and place on the baking tray. Scatter the sesame seeds all over, with a small pinch of salt and pepper. Bake for 8–10 minutes, keeping a close eye to ensure they don't burn. When golden brown and crisp, remove from the oven and transfer to a cooling rack. They will continue to crisp as they cool.

Not suitable for freezing

braised wild mushroom broth

Braising wild mushrooms gently coaxes out enough flavour without stripping them of their character — a simple but effective way to preserve their delicacy and beauty. If you can't get your hands on wild mushrooms, simply use a mixture of varieties such as button, chestnut and portobello. Soda bread croutons are lovely served with this soup for a little texture and extra substance.

Serves 4 calories 58 (V/VE if using vegetable stock)

Carbs 5g   Sugar 4g   Protein 4g   Fibre 3g   Fat 2g   Sat Fat 0.3g   Salt 0.1g

½ onion, finely diced

1 celery stick, finely diced

2 medium carrots, peeled and finely diced

1 garlic clove, finely chopped

½ tablespoon olive oil

500g wild mushrooms, such as chanterelles, giroles, morels or a mixture of different kinds

2 sprigs of rosemary, leaves picked and roughly chopped (alternatively, use thyme)

1 litre beef or vegetable stock

1 sprig of tarragon (optional)

small bunch of parsley, roughly chopped, to garnish

Soda Bread Croutons, to serve (page 34)

Preheat the oven to 200°C/gas mark 6.

In an ovenproof casserole dish or saucepan, sauté the onion, celery, carrot and garlic in the olive oil and 1 tablespoon of water for 10 minutes, stirring from time to time. Add a splash more water if the vegetables stick to the pan.

Meanwhile, carefully clean the mushrooms using a soft-bristled brush or some damp kitchen paper. Add to the saucepan with the rosemary and sauté, stirring, for about 5 minutes until nicely softened.

Add the stock and tarragon (if using) and bring to the boil. Cover with a lid, and transfer to the oven for 20–25 minutes. When ready, remove the tarragon and serve garnished with some freshly chopped parsley and soda bread croutons.

Tip: To make this dairy- and gluten-free, simply leave out the soda bread croutons.

fladelsuppe (german pancake soup)

When I'm unwell, this is how I like to have my chicken broth – adorned with one of my ultimate comfort foods, pancakes. It may sound like an unusual combination, but trust me, this is the perfect soup for when you feel poorly. Delicate but wholesome chicken broth soaked up with deliciously simple yet substantial pancakes, it's perfect for boosting energy and making you feel a bit more human.

Serves 4 calories 185 (V if using vegetable stock)

Carbs 17g   Sugar 2g   Protein 7g   Fibre 0.8g   Fat 10g   Sat Fat 2.2g   Salt 0.2g

80g flour
150ml semi-skimmed milk
2 medium free-range eggs, whisked
salt and pepper
olive or rapeseed oil for frying
1.2 litres chicken stock
generous pinch of nutmeg
small bunch of chives, finely chopped

Place the flour in a medium bowl and gradually whisk in the milk and eggs, until it's the consistency of pouring cream. Season generously with salt and pepper.

Heat a medium-sized skillet or frying pan and brush with a little oil. Pour in a ladle of the pancake mix, swirling so that it spreads and covers the pan. After 3–4 minutes and once the pancake has a little colour, flip over and cook on the other side. Repeat to make 3 more pancakes.

Bring the chicken stock to the boil, season with salt, pepper and nutmeg.

Roll up the pancakes and slice into thin shreds. Divide between 4 bowls. Pour over the hot stock, garnish with chives and serve.

pea and mushroom rare beef broth

This is a real feel-good soup, celebrating the flavour, texture and pure, unadulterated nutrition of barely cooked meat and vegetables. To make this soup vegetarian, simply replace the beef with some firm tofu.

Serves 4 calories 115 DF GF

Carbs 6.5g   Sugar 2.5g   Protein 12.3g   Fibre 2.7g   Fat 3.8g   Sat Fat 1.1g   Salt 1.3g

1.2 litres Mushroom Stock (page 16)

2 tablespoons sweet white miso paste

1 tablespoon tamari or light soy sauce

100g edamame beans

100g sugar-snap peas, each one cut into three

4 small radishes, thinly sliced

70g enoki mushrooms, roots removed if still attached

4 baby pak choi (2 normal-sized ones will also suffice), sliced

120g beef fillet, sliced into thin strips

Bring the stock to the boil and then reduce to barely a simmer. Whisk in the miso and tamari or soy sauce and taste for seasoning.

Add all of the vegetables and simmer for no longer than 2–3 minutes. Divide between 4 bowls and top with the sliced beef. If you prefer more well-done meat, place the fillet slices in the bowl before pouring in the hot broth. This will cook the beef. Serve immediately.

Not suitable for freezing

miso soup with tofu and spring onions

Although I normally choose to serve this soup in its simplest form, once you have the base figured out, you can add pretty much anything you like. For a soup that is so deeply satisfying and flavoursome, this is about the easiest one to make. Experiment with different types of miso pastes to find your perfect flavour. You can find instant dashi in Asian supermarkets if making your own is a stretch too far.

Serves 4

Carbs 4.4g   Sugar 0.8g   Protein 7.3g   Fibre 1g   Fat 4.4g   Sat Fat 0.6g   Salt 1.3g

5g wakame seaweed

1.2 litres Japanese Dashi (page 17)

3½ tablespoons miso paste (I use 2½ tablespoons sweet white miso and 1 tablespoon barley miso)

1 teaspoon rice vinegar

200g silken tofu, drained and cubed

To garnish

4 spring onions

black sesame seeds (optional)

1 teaspoon toasted sesame oil (optional)

Soak the dried wakame in hot water for 10 minutes until soft, then cut into thin strips.

Gently heat the dashi in a medium saucepan, until just about simmering. Whisk a spoonful of hot dashi into the miso paste to loosen it, then add this to the rest of the stock, along with the vinegar. It is very important not to boil this soup as the nutritional value of miso depletes when overheated. You want to keep it at just below boiling point at all times.

Add the tofu and wakame, divide between 4 bowls and garnish with spring onions and, if using, black sesame seeds and a few drops of sesame oil.

Not suitable for freezing

hoi an new wives' broth with prawn dumplings

This is an adaptation of a recipe I learned to cook in Hoi An, Vietnam. It is traditionally served ceremonially, a new wife making it for her husband's family, and its success, or lack thereof, will signify her future success as a wife. A perfect example of how integral food is to the lives of the Vietnamese (pictured on page 66).

Serves 4 calories 159

Carbs 12.5g   Sugar 12g   Protein 17g   Fibre 8g   Fat 2.5g   Sat Fat 0.4g   Salt 4g

For the stock
1 small savoy cabbage
2 teaspoons fish sauce
½ teaspoon palm sugar
   (or caster sugar)
½ teaspoon salt

For the prawn dumplings
4 spring onions, roughly chopped
300g fresh raw prawns
1 garlic clove, finely chopped
5g chives, finely chopped
10g coriander, roughly chopped
1 tablespoon fish sauce
½ teaspoon salt

For the soup base
½ tablespoon toasted sesame oil
   (or sunflower oil)
2 spring onions, finely chopped
1 shallot, finely chopped
80g prawn dumpling mixture
100g chestnut mushrooms,
   finely chopped

First make the stock. Remove the tough outer leaves of the cabbage, reserve two, wash and cut in half. Place in a medium saucepan with 1.8 litres of water, fish sauce, palm sugar and salt. Simmer for 20 minutes. When ready, strain and return to a medium heat to keep warm.

Meanwhile, make the dumplings. Place the spring onions into a mini food processor and blitz until finely chopped. Add the prawns, garlic, chives, coriander, fish sauce, and salt and blitz until just combined. You don't want a purée, so blitz with caution! Set aside 80g of the dumpling mix. Using wet hands, shape the rest into 16 little dumplings, weighing about 20g each. Chill in the fridge until needed. This can be done up to a day in advance.

To make the soup base, heat the sesame oil and 1 tablespoon water in a frying pan and fry the spring onions and shallot for a couple of minutes before adding the reserved dumpling mixture and mushrooms. Mix well to ensure the prawn mixture breaks down rather than cooking in chunks. Add the fish sauce, salt and pepper and fry for a further 5 minutes.

Prepare the remaining cabbage. Strip the leaves and shred as finely as possible. Bring the stock to boiling point and

1 tablespoon fish sauce
½ teaspoon salt
½ teaspoon black pepper
2 carrots, peeled and finely
sliced

Garnishes
coriander
sliced spring onions
sliced red chilli

blanch the cabbage and sliced carrots for no more than 2 minutes. Refresh under cold water and set aside. Now poach the prawn dumplings: place them into the stock when it is gently simmering and poach for 5 minutes, turning them as they cook.

To serve the soup, divide the cabbage, carrots, mushrooms and the prawn mixture between 4 bowls, along with the dumplings. Pour over the boiling stock, garnish with coriander, spring onions and sliced red chilli and serve.

Not suitable for freezing

umami broth with five-spice asparagus, pork and chive dumplings

When in Vietnam I had a soup made with ground pork fried with five-spice powder and other aromatics, served in a deliciously flavoured broth with Chinese chives and tofu. I can still close my eyes and taste every mouthful of that soup. The broth they used took twenty-four hours to make — this one takes a lot less time, but packs a powerful punch and is the perfect vehicle for the flavours I remember so distinctly.

Serves 4 calories 212

Carbs 22g   Sugar 2.2g   Protein 16.7g   Fibre 1.1g   Fat 6.1g   Sat Fat 1.7g   Salt 2.7g

For the broth
15g sun-dried tomatoes
15g porcini mushrooms
2 garlic cloves, peeled
approx. 20g Parmesan rind
4 black olives
1 bay leaf

Place all of the broth ingredients up to and including the bay leaf in a large saucepan and cover with 1.5 litres of water. Slowly bring to the boil, then simmer for about 35–40 minutes. Strain through a sieve lined with muslin or a clean J-cloth. Return to a clean saucepan and add the balsamic vinegar and fish sauce.

½ tablespoon balsamic vinegar

1½ tablespoons fish sauce

For the dumplings

175g lean pork mince

3 asparagus spears, finely
    chopped

10g chives, finely chopped

1¼ teaspoons five-spice powder

1 tablespoon tamari or dark soy
    sauce

¾ tablespoon fish sauce

1 teaspoon hoisin sauce
    (or a pinch of sugar)

generous pinch of black pepper

½ teaspoon cornflour

16 gyoza wrappers (available from
    Asian supermarkets, often in
    the freezer section)

While the stock is cooking, make the dumplings. Mix
the pork mince, asparagus, chives, five-spice powder,
tamari or soy sauce, fish sauce, hoisin, black pepper and
cornflour until thoroughly combined.

Lay out the gyoza wrappers, covering with a damp tea-
towel to stop them from drying out while you work. Have a
small bowl of cold water on standby. Holding a wrapper in
one hand, place a teaspoon of mixture (about 10g) in the
centre. Dip your fingers into the water and dampen the
edges, then fold in half to create a semi-circle, pinching
together at the top. Fold pleats along the edge of the
dumpling, pinching them together as you go to make sure
the wrapper is sealed. Place the dumpling on a baking tray
lined with parchment, cover with a damp tea-towel and
continue until all the wrappers have been filled.

Bring the stock to a very gentle simmer. Bring a separate,
very large saucepan, or wide frying pan full of water, to
the boil. Poach the gyoza dumplings for no longer than
5 minutes, flipping over after 2 minutes. Using a slotted
spoon, transfer to four bowls and cover with the hot
umami broth. Serve immediately.

Note: it is not necessary to pleat the gyoza wrappers; you
can simply seal them when folded into half-moon shapes,
if you wish.

Gyoza wrappers should not be refrozen if bought from
the freezer section; if bought fresh, it is fine to freeze the
prepared, uncooked dumplings.

Broth base suitable for freezing

spiced consommé with salmon, buckwheat noodles and kale

You get a lot of flavour for very little effort here and the ingredients require the simplest preparation. I sometimes serve this with slices of raw salmon only — an elegant and sophisticated entertaining option.

Serves 4 calories 219 (GF if using tamari)

Carbs 23g   Sugar 6.5g   Protein 16g   Fibre 1.1g   Fat 6g   Sat Fat 1.2g   Salt 2.7g

1 onion, peeled and roughly sliced

1 garlic clove, peeled

100ml tamari or dark soy sauce

1 tablespoon fennel seeds

1 tablespoon coriander seeds

1 star anise

1 cinnamon stick

3 whole cloves

5 black peppercorns

2 tablespoons shaoxing wine

1kg ripe tomatoes on the vine, roughly chopped and vines reserved

100g buckwheat noodles

200g fresh salmon fillet, sliced thinly

100g kale

lime wedges, to serve

Place a heavy-based saucepan on a high heat and char the sliced onions and garlic clove for 4–5 minutes, until they take on a little colour.

Add the tamari or soy sauce, fennel seeds, coriander seeds, star anise, cinnamon stick, cloves, peppercorns, shaoxing wine and 400ml water. Now add the chopped tomatoes, along with their vines. Don't worry if it seems like there are a lot of tomatoes for the amount of liquid — they will reduce in size as they release their juices and soften. Give everything a good stir, place the lid on the saucepan and simmer on a medium heat for 30 minutes.

When ready, mash the juice from the tomatoes using a potato masher. Strain through a very fine sieve, and leave to stand for about 15 minutes. Gently press any remaining liquid from the tomatoes and spices before discarding them.

Cook the noodles according to packet instructions. When ready to serve, pour the consommé into a medium saucepan and gently heat to just below boiling point. Add the kale and simmer for 3–4 minutes. When ready, divide the kale and warm noodles between 4 bowls, followed by the slices of salmon. Pour in the broth and serve immediately, with a few wedges of lime.

Consommé only suitable for freezing

turmeric and lemongrass shellfish bisque

This dish makes use of the Turmeric and Lemongrass Paste on page 18, teaming it with coconut water and the heads and shells of fresh king prawns to make a superbly intense bisque base for the shellfish to be served in. A real showstopper, it's a good option for entertaining as the bisque can be made ahead of time.

Serves 4

calories 141 DF GF

Carbs 7g   Sugar 6.5g   Protein 21g   Fibre 0g   Fat 3.2g   Sat Fat 1.6g   Salt 3g

80g Turmeric and Lemongrass Paste (page 18)
500ml coconut water
300g raw king prawns, heads and shells on
300g mussels
300g clams
3 tablespoons fish sauce
juice of 1 lime
2 tablespoons coconut milk
coriander or parsley, to garnish

Place the Turmeric and Lemongrass Paste, coconut water and 1.5 litres water in a large saucepan and bring to the boil. Remove the heads and shell from the prawns, add to the stock and simmer vigorously for 30 minutes. Run a sharp knife down the back of each prawn, and then use the tip of it to remove the intestinal tract. Rinse under cold water and set aside.

Wash the mussels and clams under plenty of cold water. Discard any that are slightly open but don't close when tapped firmly on the counter. Remove the tough beards protruding from the shells of the mussels along with any barnacles on the surface.

When the stock has reduced by about a third, strain it through a muslin-lined sieve (a clean J-cloth will also work). Return to the cleaned-out saucepan, season with the fish sauce and lime juice, adjusting to your taste. Add the coconut milk, followed by the shellfish. Simmer for no longer than 3–4 minutes. Serve garnished with chopped coriander or parsley.

Note: you can freeze leftover coconut milk in tablespoon measures in an ice-cube tray to prevent waste (see page 9).

Bisque suitable for freezing without fish

tomato consommé cooler

This is perfect for a sunny summer afternoon sitting in the garden. It is full of fresh, zingy flavours and textures, and there is minimal preparation and literally no cooking involved. Endeavour to make this soup when tomatoes are at the peak of their season from July to October.

Serves 4

Carbs 9.5g   Sugar 8.3g   Protein 3g   Fibre 5.3g   Fat 8g   Sat Fat 1.6g   Salt trace

For the consommé
1.5kg ripe tomatoes
1 cucumber, roughly chopped
50g basil
3 teaspoons freshly grated horseradish
1 garlic clove, peeled
2–3 tablespoons sherry vinegar
juice and zest of 1 lemon
salt, to taste
½ teaspoon black pepper

For the soup
¼ red onion
½ green pepper
½ red pepper
½ yellow pepper
1 celery stick
¼ cucumber
1 unripe avocado

To make the consommé, put the tomatoes, cucumber, basil, horseradish, garlic, sherry vinegar, lemon juice and zest, salt and pepper into a blender or food-processor and blitz until smooth. You may need to do this in batches.

Line a sieve with some muslin cloth, or a couple of clean, dry J-cloths, and place over a large bowl. Pour in the tomato consommé mixture, bring the edges of the muslin or J-cloth together and tie with a piece of string.

Place in the fridge and leave to drain for 6–8 hours or overnight. Never squeeze the mixture through the cloth to extract more juice as it will result in a cloudy consommé. This part of the recipe is suitable for freezing.

To serve, finely chop the vegetables and divide evenly between 4 bowls. Pour over the chilled liquid (straight from the fridge) and serve.

Tips: Instead of discarding the tomato pulp, simmer with a can of chopped tomatoes for 30 minutes, season with salt and pepper and freeze in batches of about 450g for a ready-made pasta sauce.

Using halves of different-coloured peppers is for visual purposes; you can, if you wish, use just one type.

tropical consommé with granita

This is a brilliant dessert option when entertaining. Serve in individual bowls, or present as one big chilled punch bowl at a summer garden party for people to help themselves. If you have any consommé left over, freeze in ice-pop moulds with the chopped fruit, or use as a base for smoothies.

Serves 4

Carbs 55g   Sugar 55g   Protein 2.5g   Fibre 7g   Fat 1.7g   Sat Fat 0.5g   Salt 0.1g

½ small watermelon
  (approx. 1.8kg)
¼ pineapple (approx. 400g)
¼ cantaloupe melon
  (approx. 550g)
1 small papaya (approx. 250g),
  deseeded and peeled
1 medium mango
seeds of ½ pomegranate
2 passion fruits, seeds scraped out
juice of 1 lime
250ml coconut water
1 teaspoon vanilla extract

To serve
seeds of remaining ½
  pomegranate
300g pineapple, finely chopped
300g melon, finely chopped
300g watermelon, deseeded and
  finely chopped
granita (see method)
a few sprigs of mint, leaves picked

Peel and roughly chop all of the fruit, deseeding the watermelon and cantaloupe melon. Place in a large bowl, along with the lime juice and blitz with a hand-held blender until the fruit is all broken down. Alternatively, use a food-processor.

Place a sieve lined with muslin or a clean J-cloth over a large bowl. Pour in the blitzed fruit, tie the edges of the cloth together, and chill in the fridge overnight.

When the consommé is ready, prepare the granita by placing the leftover fruit pulp into a plastic container with the coconut water and vanilla extract and freeze.

About 30 minutes before you are ready to serve, take the granita from the freezer and leave to soften a little. This is a good time to prepare the serving fruit. Scrape the surface of the frozen pulp using a fork to make the granita — it will resemble snow-like crystals.

Serve the consommé with the mixed chopped fruit, granita and a few leaves of fresh mint.

Note: this soup needs to be prepared in advance. Make it the night before you plan to use it, and freeze the granita the following morning. Everything will then be ready by lunchtime, and certainly by the evening.

15-minute soups

Even the keenest of cooks, myself included, will sometimes struggle to fit home cooking into their day. Furthermore, being healthy is often hampered by being busy: when we don't have time to think, to stop or even to sit down, eating becomes a grab-and-go affair, and we will often wind up making choices we regret.

The soups in this chapter are incredibly easy to whip up, and require little effort, skill or thought. So even when you're at your most exhausted at the end of a long day, they shouldn't feel unachievable. The Pea, Mint and Basil and Roasted Red Pepper, Chickpea and Herb soups, for example, include ingredients that can be kept in the freezer or store-cupboard, meaning you don't have a long shopping list before you can start. One of the simplest recipes in this book, Egg Drop Soup, is about as quick and easy as a dish can be — and surprisingly satisfying too.

Lunch can be the difference between feeling lethargic and slow or fresh and energetic. The right choice can leave you with a fresh lease of life in the middle of the day. The homemade noodle pot recipes in this chapter are designed for you to take to work, and with little more than the addition of boiling hot water, you have a nutritious, filling, satisfying and generally feel-good lunch on your hands.

It is important to note that the timing for the soups in this chapter starts from the moment you start cooking, not chopping. However, as they are easy and straightforward, the preparation won't be laborious. Also, the first step in most of these recipes is to boil the stock — this is a simple time-saving trick, which has your veggies cooking as soon as they are submerged in liquid.

the quickest tomato soup

Few things can beat a good tomato soup, and having a fail-proof recipe in your repertoire — especially one that only takes minutes to make — will stand you in good stead. The recipe accounts for those times when tomatoes are not in season, or when really good ones are hard to come by, but if making it when they are in season, use all fresh.

Serves 4   (V/VE if using vegetable stock)

Carbs 10g   Sugar 9.5g   Protein 1.7g   Fibre 2.7g   Fat 2g   Sat Fat 0.3g   Salt 0.1g

500ml vegetable or chicken stock
2 celery sticks, halved
1 carrot, halved
1 small onion
1 garlic clove
½ tablespoon olive oil
500g mixed tomatoes, such
    as beef, plum and cherry,
    roughly chopped
1 x 400g can plum tomatoes
1 tablespoon red wine vinegar
salt and pepper

In a small saucepan, bring the stock to the boil. Place the celery, carrot, onion and garlic into a hand-held mini blender and blitz until roughly chopped. Transfer to a medium saucepan with the olive oil and 1 tablespoon of water and sauté for a couple of minutes. Add the chopped tomatoes and cook for 2–3 minutes longer, followed by the tinned tomatoes and stock.

Simmer for 10 minutes. Add the red wine vinegar, blitz until smooth and season to taste with salt and pepper.

Serve with Roasted Cherry Tomato Rye Bruschetta (page 80), if you're able to eat gluten. Alternatively serve just the roasted tomatoes as a garnish for this soup.

Tip: As the calorie content of this soup is so low, you can afford to be a little indulgent. Make a cream of tomato soup by adding 75ml cream once the soup has been blitzed. The soup will then be 105 calories per portion, but won't be dairy-free. You can also add a bunch of basil before blending to create a basil and tomato soup.

roasted cherry tomato rye bruschetta

Nothing beats the punchy flavour of a roasted tomato — it needs little more than some simple seasoning. I have added a splash of sherry vinegar. If you don't have this, balsamic is a good alternative. Equally, if you don't have either this recipe won't suffer, so don't fret.

Serves 4 calories 75

Carbs 13g   Sugar 2.6g   Protein 2.7g   Fibre 2.5g   Fat 0.7g   Sat Fat 0.1g   Salt 0.4g

300g cherry tomatoes on
   the vine
1 teaspoon sherry vinegar
   (optional)
4 thin slices Pumpkin Seed and
   Prune Rye Soda Bread
   (page 32)
1 garlic clove, peeled (optional)
basil, to garnish
salt and pepper

Preheat the oven to 240°C/gas mark 9 or to its highest setting. Place the tomatoes on a baking tray with the sherry vinegar, if using, and roast for 10–15 minutes.

Toast the bread. Rub the garlic, if using, all over each slice of toast. Gently remove the tomatoes from the vine, place 4–5 on each slice of bread and use the back of a fork to squash them, releasing their juices. Garnish with some freshly torn basil, salt and pepper before serving.

homemade lunch noodle pots

fresh veg pot with soy broth, chicken and pickled ginger

As this and the other noodle pot recipes are designed to bring to work, each recipe serves one. To avoid wasting leftover ingredients, I'd advise making one recipe a few days in a row. Furthermore, there are no hard-and-fast rules here — use whatever ingredients you have to hand, or simply prefer.

Serves 1

Carbs 8.5g   Sugar 4.2g   Protein 14.7g   Fibre 2.5g   Fat 6.7g   Sat Fat 1.3g   Salt 2.2g

3 tablespoons tamari or dark soy sauce
½ tablespoon fish sauce
½ tablespoon mirin
juice of ½ lime
100g or 7 little nests of konnyaku shirataki noodles, rinsed
60g cooked chicken breast, sliced
1 small pak choi, quartered lengthways
¼ carrot, julienned or grated
15g kale
50g red cabbage, thinly sliced
2 sprigs of Thai basil, leaves picked (optional)
2 sprigs of mint, leaves picked
1 red bird's eye chilli, thinly sliced (optional)
a few slices of pickled sushi ginger (available in lots of supermarkets, Asian stores and online)

Mix the tamari or soy sauce, fish sauce, mirin and lime juice in your soup container, such as a jam jar or small tupperware box. Add the noodles and mix well. Now add the remaining ingredients and refrigerate until ready to use. When ready, cover with about 300ml of boiling water, stir everything together and leave to stand for 5 minutes before eating.

All noodle pot recipes not suitable for freezing

salmon and veg noodle pot with korean gochujang broth

Serves 1

Carbs 7g   Sugar 4.2g   Protein 14.7g   Fibre 1.1g   Fat 6.5g   Sat Fat 1.3g   Salt 2.2g

1 tablespoon gochujang
1 tablespoon tamari or light soy sauce
juice of 1 lime
100g or 7 little nests of konnyaku shirataki
  noodles, rinsed
15g kale
20g red cabbage, finely sliced
¼ celery stick, finely sliced
1 small spring onion, finely sliced
60g fresh salmon, sliced into thin strips
3–4 sprigs of coriander, leaves picked
lime wedge, to serve

Mix the gochujang, tamari or soy sauce and lime juice in your soup container until it is a smooth paste. Add the noodles and mix well. Now add all of the vegetables, salmon, coriander and lime wedge. Refrigerate until ready to use. Remove the lime wedge, cover with about 300ml of boiling water, give a little stir to separate the noodles, and leave to stand for 5 minutes. Add a squeeze of lime juice before eating.

walnut miso noodle broth with fennel, radish and enoki mushrooms

Serves 1

Carbs 12g   Sugar 5g   Protein 6g   Fibre 2.6g   Fat 3g   Sat Fat 0.2g   Salt 4g

20g Walnut Miso Paste (page 18)
1½ tablespoons tamari or light soy sauce
100g or 7 little nests of konnyaku shirataki
  noodles, rinsed
50g fennel, thinly sliced
2 small radishes, thinly sliced
½ teaspoon lemon juice
15g edamame beans
40g whole enoki mushrooms (or plain
  button mushrooms, thinly sliced)
1 teaspoon chives, finely chopped

Mix the Walnut Miso Paste with the tamari or soy sauce in the container for your soup. Place the noodles on top and mix well. Slice the fennel and radishes as thinly as possible (a mandolin is best for this) and dress with a little lemon juice. Add to the container, along with the edamame beans, mushrooms and chives. Refrigerate until ready to use, then cover with 300ml boiling water. Stir gently to separate the noodles, and leave to stand for 5 minutes before eating.

lettuce and gorgonzola with basil

You can play around with the type of lettuce you use here to experiment with the overall flavour. I love to use bitter chicory, which compliments and balances the creaminess of gorgonzola. When I blend this soup I avoid making it completely smooth, as I love the texture of the half blended crunchy lettuce. This is great with the Beetroot, Chive and Sumac Buckwheat Tortilla (page 99).

Serves 4   (V if using vegetable stock)

Carbs 3g   Sugar 2g   Protein 4.5g   Fibre 2.6g   Fat 6g   Sat Fat 3g   Salt 0.6g

750ml vegetable or chicken stock
1 small leek, finely sliced
1 celery stick, roughly diced
1 garlic clove, roughly chopped
½ tablespoon olive oil
450g mixed lettuce leaves
   (such as baby gem, chicory,
   romaine), roughly chopped
50g gorgonzola cheese
30g basil
juice of 1 lemon
salt and pepper

Place the stock in a saucepan and bring to the boil.

Sauté the leek, celery and garlic in the olive oil and 1 tablespoon water for 4–5 minutes, until slightly softened. Add the lettuce and boiling stock. Don't worry that the stock doesn't cover the lettuce, as it heats the water the lettuce will wilt. Use the back of a wooden spoon to push the leaves down into the liquid. Simmer for about 8 minutes.

Add the gorgonzola and basil and blitz, leaving a little texture. Stir in the lemon juice, season to taste and serve.

pea, mint and basil

This soup is all about the vibrant flavours of the peas and fresh herbs, and they need little more than an onion to get things going. For an Asian twist, add ¼ teaspoon of chilli flakes when cooking the onion, and substitute basil with Thai basil. If you have time, this soup is delicious served with Peppered Sweet Potato Crisps (page 45).

Serves 4

Carbs 13g   Sugar 12g   Protein 23g   Fibre 5g   Fat 3.3g   Sat Fat 0.7g   Salt 6.8g

600ml vegetable stock
1 small onion, chopped
½ tablespoon olive oil
700g frozen peas
30g basil, leaves picked
25g mint, leaves picked
salt and pepper

Bring the stock to the boil in a saucepan.

Sauté the onion in the olive oil and 1 tablespoon water for 2–3 minutes. Add the peas, followed by the boiling stock and cook for 10 minutes. Add the herbs, blend until smooth and season to taste.

roasted red pepper, chickpea and herb

Many of the ingredients in this soup can be kept in your store-cupboard for when you need a convenient and tasty supper. Only buy roasted red peppers preserved in water and vinegar, not oil, and splash out on a good-quality jar. Remember, they are the hero of your soup, and cheaper versions can have an almost unpalatable vinegary flavour. I have used passata as the base for this soup as the sweetness of the peppers calls for an acidic counterbalance.

Serves 4   (GF if using GF stock cube)

Carbs 22g   Sugar 7.5g   Protein 8g   Fibre 10g   Fat 10g   Sat Fat 0.6g   Salt 1.9g

680ml passata

1 vegetable stock cube

1 small red onion, finely chopped

2 garlic cloves, finely chopped

1 medium red pepper, diced

½ teaspoon smoked paprika

½ tablespoon olive oil

450g jar roasted red peppers, drained and chopped into bite-sized pieces

1 x 400g can of chickpeas, drained and rinsed

salt and pepper

large bunch of basil, roughly chopped

2 sprigs of thyme, leaves picked

2 sprigs marjoram, leaves picked and chopped

Place the passata, stock cube and 200ml water in a small saucepan and bring to the boil.

Meanwhile, in another saucepan, sauté the red onion, garlic, red pepper and smoked paprika in the oil and 1 tablespoon of water, for 5 minutes. Add more water if the mixture sticks to the pan.

Add the roasted red peppers, chickpeas and boiling passata. Simmer for 10 minutes.

When ready, season with salt if you feel you need it – you may not after using the stock cube – and lots of black pepper. Stir in the herbs and serve.

korean kimchi with tofu

Native to Korea, kimchi is basically fermented vegetables, usually cabbage, and is deliciously spicy and sour. Although you can make your own, I tend to buy it from my local Asian supermarket or online.

Serves 4

calories 164 GF V

Carbs 5g   Sugar 4g   Protein 8.5g   Fibre 4.5g   Fat 11g   Sat Fat 2.5g   Salt 1.7g

400g cabbage kimchi

½ tablespoon sesame oil, plus extra to serve

1 medium onion, finely chopped

2 garlic cloves, finely chopped

2 tablespoons gochujang (Korean chilli paste)

1 tablespoon mirin

150g firm tofu, cut into 2cm cubes

4 free-range egg yolks (optional)

2 spring onions, sliced

1 tablespoons black sesame seeds

Remove the kimchi from its packaging and squeeze out any juice, reserving for later.

Heat the sesame oil in a medium saucepan and sauté the onion, garlic and kimchi on a medium heat for 3–4 minutes adding a splash of water if necessary.

Stir in the gochujang, mirin and reserved kimchi juice, followed by 1 litre of water and bring to the boil. Reduce to a simmer and cook gently for 10 minutes. Remove from the heat and add the tofu.

Serve in bowls, with an egg yolk (if using) resting on top, and garnish with spring onions, black sesame seeds and a drizzle of sesame oil.

Tip: to make this soup vegan, simply leave out the egg yolk.

Not suitable for freezing

fennel, celery and cucumber broth with coriander, mint and lime pesto

This soup is all about invigorating, sharp, clean and crisp flavours. Next to no cooking is required, as its preparation is simple. A spoonful of the coriander, mint and lime pesto stirred through the broth makes it even more special! The pesto is best made using a pestle and mortar. A 15g serving is sufficient for one person adorning a soup and any leftovers can be frozen in an ice-cube tray for use at a later time.

Serves 4

Carbs 1.7g Sugar 2g Protein 2g Fibre 2g Fat 0.7g Sat Fat 0g Salt trace

1.2 litres vegetable stock
1 small fennel bulb
4 celery sticks
2 garlic cloves, peeled
8 black peppercorns
1 sprig of mint
150g cucumber

For the Coriander, Mint and Lime Pesto (17 calories per serving: makes 120g; serves 8)
20g mint, leaves picked
20g coriander
1 garlic clove, peeled
15g whole almonds
1½ tablespoons olive oil
juice of 2 limes
salt and pepper

Boil the vegetable stock in a medium saucepan. Quarter the fennel, remove the tough outer layer and add this to the stock along with 1 stick of celery, the garlic, peppercorns and mint. Allow to simmer while you prepare the vegetables.

If you have a mandolin, or food processor with a slice attachment, thinly slice the fennel quarters, remaining celery and cucumber. Otherwise do this by hand.

Strain the stock, return to the pan and reduce the heat so that it is just below a simmer. Add the sliced vegetables and cook for 5 minutes.

Meanwhile, make the pesto. Roughly chop the herbs and add to the mortar with the garlic and almonds. Pound until you have a rough paste. Add the oil and lime juice, mix well and season with salt and pepper.

When the soup is ready, top with a spoonful of pesto. Serve immediately.

Soup not suitable for freezing

egg drop soup

When I think of fast food, I think of eggs. Nothing can be prepared more quickly, in so many different ways, and be so utterly satisfying and good for you. This soup is the essence of simplicity. You can flavour the stock if you wish, allowing it to simmer for a few minutes with a few cloves, some star anise and a cinnamon stick. You could also stir through a few tablespoons of sweet white miso. To make this for one, use about 300ml stock and 1 whole egg.

Serves 4   (GF if using homemade chicken stock; V if using vegetable stock)

calories 75

Carbs 1.7g   Sugar 0.6g   Protein 6g   Fibre 0.2g   Fat 5g   Sat Fat 1.3g   Salt 0.2g

1.2 litres chicken or vegetable stock, preferably homemade
salt and pepper
1 teaspoon cornflour
3 free-range eggs
3 spring onions, sliced

Bring the chicken stock to the boil, and reduce the heat so that it is barely simmering – it is important not to pour the eggs into a boiling stock. Taste and season to your liking in order to create a strong base for the remaining ingredients.

Mix the cornflour with a little water to form a smooth paste and then whisk in the eggs. Season with salt and pepper.

Pour the eggs into the stock in a very thin steady stream using a whisk to gently incorporate them. As soon as the eggs have been added, remove from the heat and leave to stand for a minute or two. The soup will have a slightly curdled effect, but this is how it should look, so don't worry. Serve immediately, garnished with spring onions.

Not suitable for freezing

broccoli and ginger with yogurt, cucumber and mint

Both broccoli and ginger are packed with antioxidants, and each boasts its own collection of vitamins and nutrients to make this soup a real cracker. There is a very gentle heat from the chilli and ginger, which is beautifully counterbalanced by the addition of some cooling cucumber, yogurt and mint.

Serves 4

Carbs 10g   Sugar 6.5g   Protein 7g   Fibre 5.5g   Fat 3g   Sat Fat 1.7g   Salt 0.2g

200ml coconut water
700ml boiling vegetable stock
4 spring onions, tough green tips
    removed and roughly chopped
I garlic clove, roughly chopped
30g ginger, peeled and grated
I green chilli, seeds removed and
    roughly chopped
½ teaspoon garam masala
½ tablespoon coconut oil
500g head of broccoli, broken
    into very small florets and
    stalks roughly chopped
salt and pepper

To serve
2 tablespoons natural yogurt
¼ cucumber, deseeded and
    finely grated or chopped
a few sprigs of mint, leaves picked
    and finely chopped

Add the coconut water to the stock and bring to the boil.

Sauté the spring onions, garlic, ginger, chilli and garam masala in the coconut oil and I tablespoon of water on a medium heat for 2–3 minutes, stirring occasionally.

Add the broccoli, followed by the boiling stock and coconut water. Turn the heat right up so that it boils quickly, then reduce the heat and simmer for 8 minutes.

Blend the soup until smooth and season to taste. Serve topped with yogurt, cucumber and mint.

mushroom soup with a kick

This spicy, salty, earthy soup is refreshingly unpredictable. It has a real depth of flavour which bounces around your palate and leaves behind a smacking warmth that will have you chilli lovers coming back for more (if you are not a spice lover, feel free to leave out the chillies). Don't fuss over chopping the mushrooms, simply tear them into the pot to save on time.

Serves 4   (V/VE if using vegetable stock)

calories 60 DF GF

Carbs 4g   Sugar 3.5g   Protein 6g   Fibre 2g   Fat 2g   Sat Fat 0.3g   Salt 2.2g

750ml vegetable, mushroom or beef stock

1 red onion, sliced

2 garlic cloves, roughly sliced

2 bay leaves

3 sprigs of thyme, leaves picked

2 sprigs of rosemary, leaves picked and roughly chopped

1 small red chilli, roughly chopped (seeds removed if you prefer less heat)

½ tablespoon olive oil

700g chestnut mushrooms, roughly torn into chunks

2 tablespoons tamari or light soy sauce

salt and pepper

Bring the stock to the boil. Sauté the onion, garlic, bay leaves, thyme, rosemary and chilli in the olive oil and 1 tablespoon water, on a medium heat for 5 minutes.

Add the mushrooms and stock and boil for 10 minutes. Remove the bay leaves, then add the tamari or soy sauce and blend until smooth. Season to taste. You won't need much salt, if any, as the soy sauce is naturally salty.

Note: mushrooms can be reluctant to break down so you need to persevere, if using a stick blender, to achieve a smooth consistency.

buckwheat tortillas done three ways

When we think soup, big chunks of crusty bread come to mind as an accompaniment. These flavoursome buckwheat tortillas provide the same bit of substance without weighing you down the way that bread can. You can slice them and use them to scoop up soup or fill them like a wrap and serve alongside a soup for a more filling meal. Feel free to experiment.

Walnut Miso and Spring Onion

Serves 4   GF DF V

Carbs 17g   Sugar 1g   Protein 2g   Fibre 0.7g   Fat 4g   Sat Fat 0.3g   Salt 0.3g

75g buckwheat flour
1 egg white
40g Walnut Miso Paste (page 18)
3 spring onions, finely sliced
salt and pepper
rapeseed oil, for frying

Whisk the flour, egg white and 200ml water until you have a smooth batter, similar in consistency to pouring cream. Add the remaining ingredients and season generously.

Heat a skillet or heavy-based frying pan and brush with a little rapeseed oil. Pour in a ladleful of batter and spread around the pan. Cook for 3–4 minutes on each side and repeat with the remaining batter. Serve with Pea, Mint and Basil Soup (page 87) or Broccoli and Ginger Soup (page 96).

Beetroot, Chive and Sumac

Serves 4   DF GF V

Carbs 16g   Sugar 1g   Protein 2.7g   Fibre 0.9g   Fat 3g   Sat Fat 0.2g   Salt 0.1g

75g buckwheat flour
1 egg white
1 raw beetroot, grated
5g chives, finely chopped
½ teaspoon sumac
salt and pepper
rapeseed oil, for frying

Follow the instructions above.

Serve with Lettuce and Gorgonzola Soup with Basil (page 85) or Fennel, Celery and Cucumber Broth with Coriander, Mint and Lime Pesto (page 92)

Courgette, Feta Cheese and Thyme

Serves 4 calories 116 GF V

Carbs 16g · Sugar 0.5g · Protein 3.6g · Fibre 0.8g · Fat 4g · Sat Fat 0.9g · Salt 0.2g

75g buckwheat flour
1 egg white
1 small courgette, grated
20g feta cheese
4 sprigs of thyme, leaves picked
salt and pepper
rapeseed oil, for frying

Follow the instructions on page 99.

Serve with Chunky Courgette and Dill with Prawns (page 102), Mushroom Soup with a Kick (page 98) or Roasted Red Pepper, Chickpea and Herb (page 88).

A note on buckwheat flour

This flour is gluten-free and has a deliciously delicate, earthy flavour. It's worth keeping in the store-cupboard, as the tortillas won't work or taste the same using plain flour. It's available in big supermarkets, health-food shops and online.

chunky courgette and dill with prawns

This soup boasts a lot of flavour for the little time and effort it takes to make. It's important to use fresh prawns here and even more important not to overcook them.

Serves 4 calories 88 DF GF

Carbs 4.5g Sugar 3g Protein 11g Fibre 2.5g Fat 2.5g Sat Fat 0.5g Salt 0.3g

600ml vegetable or chicken stock
½ tablespoon olive oil
1 medium leek, halved and sliced into half-moons, about 5mm thick
3 medium courgettes, halved and sliced into half-moons about 5mm thick
½ teaspoon chilli flakes (optional)
zest and juice of ½ lime
20g dill, fronds picked from the stalks and chopped
175g raw shelled prawns
salt and pepper

Boil the stock in a medium saucepan. Heat the oil in another saucepan and sauté the leek and courgettes with 1 tablespoon water for about 4 minutes, stirring occasionally.

Add the boiling stock and simmer for a further 5 minutes. Add the chilli flakes and lime zest and juice. Remove half of the soup and blend with half of the dill until smooth. Return to the saucepan, add the prawns and cook for no more than 3 minutes, until they have turned pink.

Just before serving, stir through the remaining dill. Season to taste and serve immediately.

Not suitable for freezing

Note: serve with Courgette, Feta Cheese and Thyme or Walnut Miso and Spring Onion buckwheat tortillas (pages 99–100).

grains and pulses

The variety of grains and pulses available to us is vast and at times overwhelming. However, they are without doubt one of the healthiest food groups. Each has its own distinctive, sometimes delicate, at other times more punchy flavour. They are full of good things such as protein and fibre, give a slow release of energy, fill us up for longer, are generally easy to cook and are mostly very affordable. Furthermore, their uses reach far beyond the soup recipes in this book, making them a sensible store-cupboard staple: teamed with wild mushrooms, pearl barley makes a great risotto; mixed with some olive oil, tahini, garlic and lemon, chickpeas will transform into a decadent hummus; and quinoa is a great all-rounder, as comfortable in granola and cakes as it is in salads, soups and stews.

This chapter showcases how versatile grains and pulses can be, ranging from Mexican Posole Verde Soup to the more traditional Caramelised Onion, Pearl Barley and Cavolo Nero soup. Freekeh is a perfect demonstration of how flavoursome a grain can be, boasting aromas and flavours not dissimilar to smoky bacon. Cannellini beans make a creamy smooth-textured soup base for pomegranate and tahini-roasted broccoli (see page 118), while they can also be served as a garnish, creating texture and interest. Chickpeas are converted into deep purple roasted jewels for a simple but delicious watercress soup.

The recipes in this chapter are among the most filling in the book, and generally have a calorie content closer to the 300 mark. They work brilliantly as a more substantial meal option, and will not only fill you up, but will keep you going too. These are a fantastic example of how, as we would say in Ireland, 'There is eatin' and drinkin' in that soup.'

carrot, rhubarb and yellow lentil

Carrot and rhubarb may seem an odd combination, but the sour rhubarb complements the sweet carrots and the result is a rather lovely, subtle flavour of both.

Serves 4   (V/VE if using vegetable stock)

Carbs 20g   Sugar 10.5g   Protein 12g   Fibre 9g   Fat 2.5g   Sat Fat 0.6g   Salt 0.4g

2 banana shallots, finely chopped
25g ginger, finely chopped
½ tablespoon olive oil
500g carrots, peeled and roughly diced
75g yellow split lentils
I star anise
2 cardamom pods
750ml vegetable or chicken stock
250g pink rhubarb, roughly chopped
salt and pepper

Sauté the shallot and ginger in the olive oil and I tablespoon of water for about 5 minutes, adding a splash more water if necessary.

Add the carrots, lentils, star anise, cardamom and stock. Bring to the boil and cook for 15 minutes. Add the rhubarb and cook for a further IO minutes, or until the carrots are tender.

When ready, remove the spices and blitz until smooth. Add a little more water or stock if the soup is too thick. Season to taste and serve with Health-kick Crackers or Savoury Granola (page IO8).

Note: a spoonful of sweet white miso would add another flavour dimension to this soup, or add a drizzle of Coriander, Mint and Lime Pesto (page 92).

health-kick crackers
and savoury granola

The crunch of a cracker, and the texture provided by a sprinkling of savoury granola can really transform a soup. Both are really nutritious, and you could add a variety of flavours too if you are feeling a bit fancy. Herbs such as rosemary and thyme work well, as do all dried spices.

Makes 25 crackers

Carbs 1.8g   Sugar 0.1g   Protein 1.4g   Fibre 0.7g   Fat 2.4g   Sat Fat 0.4g   Salt 0.2g

70g pumpkin seeds
50g sunflower seeds
50g golden linseeds
35g black sesame seeds
2 teaspoons sea salt
100g jumbo oats
2 tablespoons tahini
2 soft pitted prunes

2 large baking trays

Preheat the oven to 150°C/gas mark 2. Place all the seeds, the sea salt and 30g of the jumbo oats in a medium bowl. Using a mini hand-held blender, blitz the remaining oats to a fine powder. Add to the bowl with the rest of the ingredients and mix well.

Blend the tahini, prunes and 130ml of water until smooth. Mix with the dry ingredients until you have sticky dough.

Divide the mixture in half and roll out each half as thinly as possible between 2 sheets of baking parchment.

Place the rolled-out mixture on two baking trays and remove the top layer of baking parchment. Bake for 20–25 minutes, until dry, crisp and golden brown. Leave to cool completely. Break one batch into 25 crackers and crumble the other to make a savoury garnish for soups and salads.

Store for up to 2 weeks in an airtight container.

Mexican posole verde (celebration soup)

There are times when soup deserves its place centre stage, and I can think of nothing nicer than sitting down to a big pot of this vibrant and invigorating soup, with all kinds of garnishes served alongside. It is perfect for a celebration! For a list of stockists for ingredients in this recipe, see page 156.

Serves 6 calories 208 GF

Carbs 17g   Sugar 7g   Protein 18g   Fibre 5g   Fat 6.5g   Sat Fat 2g   Salt 0.7g

2 small chicken breasts (approx. 300g)
400ml chicken stock
650g tomatillos, papery skins removed, washed and halved (alternatively use tinned)
5 spring onions
2 jalapeño peppers
2 poblano chillies
5 garlic cloves
juice of 2 limes
45g coriander
350g canned hominy

For the garnishes
100g avocado, diced and dressed with a little lemon or lime juice
4 pink radishes, finely sliced
10g coriander
small handful of cherry tomatoes, quartered
3 tablespoons soured cream

Place the chicken breasts in a saucepan and cover with the chicken stock. Bring to the boil, reduce to a simmer and poach for 10–12 minutes. Remove the chicken and leave to cool, then slice thinly. Set the stock aside to cool.

Place the tomatillos, spring onions, jalapeño peppers, poblano chillies, garlic, lime juice, coriander and 200g of the hominy in a blender with the reserved chicken stock and blitz until very smooth. You may need to do this in batches. You can make the soup up to this point a day in advance and keep refrigerated.

When you are ready to serve, prepare your chosen garnishes. Pour the soup into a large saucepan, add the remaining 150g of hominy, gently bring to the boil and quickly reduce the heat. It's important not to overheat or boil it as the colour will quickly diminish. When ready, taste for seasoning and bring to the table with a ladle for people to help themselves. Serve with the garnishes and sliced chicken.

Tip: Other garnishes you can also choose are spring onions, finely chopped red onion, sweetcorn, lime wedges, Health-kick Crackers or Savoury Granola (opposite).

greek chicken and lemon with dill

Native to Greece and known as Avgolemono, this soup uses egg yolks as a thickening agent and to create richness. It is a masterclass in simplicity, but for it to work you need to use the best ingredients you can get your hands on.

Serves 4

Carbs 19g   Sugar 1.3g   Protein 29g   Fibre 1.2g   Fat 11g   Sat Fat 3g   Salt 0.6g

1 litre chicken stock
600g chicken thighs, bone in and skin removed (about 5 chicken thighs, amounting to approx. 275g meat when cooked)
100g orzo pasta
2 free-range egg yolks
juice of 1 lemon (about 30ml)
salt and pepper
3 sprigs of fresh dill

Bring the chicken stock to the boil and add the chicken. Reduce to a simmer and cook for 12 minutes, skimming any fat that rises to the surface. Add the pasta after 4 minutes.

After 12 minutes, when the chicken is cooked, remove and leave to cool slightly. Reduce the heat so that the stock and orzo are just below simmering point. Whisk 3–4 tablespoons of the hot stock into the egg yolks (don't be tempted to add the eggs straight to the soup – they will curdle), then add to the stock and stir through.

Cook for 3–4 minutes over a very gentle heat – you don't want to boil the soup now as it will separate. As you stir the soup it thicken slightly, becoming similar in consistency to double cream. Add the lemon juice and season to taste. Shred the chicken, discarding the bones, and add to the soup, along with the dill, and serve immediately.

Note: this soup is best eaten fresh.

Not suitable for freezing

roasted tomato, harissa and pomegranate black bean

This is a blend of sharp pomegranate, sour tomatoes and fiery, aromatic harissa all brought together under a blanket of silken black beans. Use your own spice gauge for this soup — one whole tablespoon of rose harissa will give you a considerable smack of heat, so only use half a tablespoon if you prefer a more delicate spicing.

Serves 4 calories 128 DF GF (V/VE if using vegetable stock)

Carbs 19.5g   Sugar 8.7g   Protein 6g   Fibre 7.7g   Fat 1.2g   Sat Fat 0.2g   Salt 0.2g

1 teaspoon cumin seeds

1 teaspoon coriander seeds

1 tablespoon rose harissa

1½ tablespoons pomegranate molasses

1 tablespoon tomato purée

3 garlic cloves, finely chopped

2 teaspoons chopped fresh oregano (use dried if you can't find fresh)

juice of 1 lime

½ teaspoon black pepper

600g tomatoes on the vine, each cut into 8 wedges

400ml beef or vegetable stock

1 x 400g can black beans

2 tablespoons soured cream (optional – dish won't be dairy-free or vegan if used)

fresh pomegranate seeds to garnish (optional)

Preheat the oven to 200°C/gas mark 6. Place a small frying pan on a medium heat and toast the cumin and coriander seeds for a couple of minutes, or until fragrant and just beginning to pop. Grind to a fine powder in a pestle and mortar.

Mix the ground spices, harissa, pomegranate molasses, tomato purée, garlic, oregano, lime juice and black pepper in a medium bowl with 1 tablespoon water. Add the tomatoes, coat with the marinade, transfer to a shallow ovenproof casserole dish and roast for 30 minutes, checking and turning halfway through.

Shortly before the tomatoes are ready, bring the stock to the boil. Remove the casserole from the oven and add the black beans, along with their juices, and the boiling stock. Give everything a good stir, cover with a lid or tight layer of tinfoil, return to the oven and cook for 15 minutes.

When ready, taste for seasoning and serve with soured cream and fresh pomegranate seeds to garnish.

Garnish not suitable for freezing

broad bean, freekeh and smoked mackerel

Freekeh packs a real punch of flavour. The grains are very absorbent, so you may have to add a little more water or stock as you cook. I mostly use frozen broad beans for this, but, if they are in season, it is nice to use fresh. Skinning them is worth the effort, but if you are strapped for time the world won't come crashing down if you leave them as they are!

Serves 4 calories 180

Carbs 16g   Sugar 4.6g   Protein 8g   Fibre 5g   Fat 8g   Sat Fat 1.6g   Salt 0.5g

2 banana shallots, finely chopped
1 garlic clove, finely chopped
2 carrots, diced
½ tablespoon olive oil
50g freekeh, rinsed
100g smoked mackerel, skin removed
200g frozen broad beans, defrosted and skinned
15g dill (optional)
salt and pepper
1 lemon, sliced into 4 wedges

Sauté the shallots, garlic and carrots in the olive oil and 1 tablespoon of water for 10 minutes, stirring occasionally. Add a splash more water if the vegetables stick to the pan. Add the freekeh along with 1 litre of water. Bring to the boil and simmer with the lid on for 20–25 minutes.

If the grains have absorbed too much of the water, add a little more to achieve a brothy consistency and bring back to the boil. Flake the smoked mackerel into the soup in bite-sized pieces and simmer for about 5 minutes. Add the broad beans, then remove from the heat. You only want to heat the broad beans through, to keep them as fresh, green and crunchy as possible. Stir in the chopped dill if using, check for seasoning and serve with a wedge of lemon.

Note: if you can't find freekeh, use brown rice instead. Check cooking times on the packet and use vegetable or chicken stock instead of water.

Not suitable for freezing

A note on freekeh

Freekeh boasts three times the amount of fibre and protein as brown rice and has a smoky, almost bacon-like flavour. It is made from early harvested wheat, which results in a grain that is slightly green in colour. So assertive is its flavour, that when used in soups, there is no need for stock. It is also a fantastic base for salads. You will most likely find it in supermarket aisles, but, failing that, health-food shops are almost certain to sell it.

caramelised onion, pearl barley and cavolo nero

Onions find their way into almost all of our kitchens, but will rarely be the star of their own show. Slowly sautéed, as they are here, they change into a silky, robustly flavoured, caramelised version of themselves — moreishly rich, succulent, earthy and sweet. This soup epitomises the beauty that lies in some of our most everyday ingredients.

Serves 4   (V/VE if using Mushroom Stock and vegetarian Worcestershire sauce)

Carbs 33g Sugar 19g Protein 12g Fibre 6.5g Fat 3.6g Sat Fat 0.5g Salt 0.6g

900g onions (unpeeled weight)
½ tablespoon olive oil
2 tablespoons Worcestershire sauce
500ml beef stock (or use Mushroom Stock, page 16)
1 tablespoon finely chopped rosemary
1 tablespoon finely chopped thyme
1 tablespoon finely chopped marjoram (optional)
50g pearl barley
300ml unsweetened soya milk
70g cavolo nero (savoy cabbage will suffice)
salt and pepper

Halve, peel and trim the onions. If you have a food-processor, use the slicing blade to prepare them, otherwise, thinly slice by hand. Add to a large heavy-based casserole dish or frying pan along with the oil, Worcestershire sauce and 2 tablespoons of the beef stock. Give the onions a good stir, then cover and sauté for 50 minutes, adding the herbs halfway through. Check regularly, stirring each time. Add a splash of beef stock or water if the onions stick to the pan. It is important not to burn them.

Meanwhile, rinse the pearl barley under cold water until the water runs clear. Place in a medium saucepan, cover with 250ml water and simmer for 25–30 minutes. If the barley has absorbed all the water before it is fully cooked, simply add a little more water. When ready, drain and set aside.

When the onions are soft and a deep brown colour, add the stock and pearl barley and simmer for 10 minutes. Add the soya milk, along with the cavolo nero, and heat until just at boiling point. Generously season before serving.

cannellini bean with pomegranate and tahini-roasted broccoli

The base of this soup is very subtle – velvety smooth and light – providing a delicate base for the more intensely flavoured roasted broccoli garnish, salty from the soy sauce and sour from pomegranate molasses. The broccoli in this recipe also makes a perfect addition to salads.

Serves 4 calories 215 DF GF (V/VE if using vegetable stock)

Carbs 23g   Sugar 10g   Protein 11g   Fibre 11.5g   Fat 6g   Sat Fat 1g   Salt 1g

1½ tablespoons tahini

¾ tablespoons pomegranate molasses

2 tablespoons tamari or light soy sauce

400g head of broccoli, broken into small florets and stalks roughly chopped

½ tablespoon olive oil

1 small onion, finely chopped

1 garlic clove, finely sliced

1 small carrot, finely chopped

25g ginger, peeled and grated

¼ teaspoon chilli flakes

240g cannellini beans (1 x 400g can, drained)

800ml vegetable or chicken stock

45g pomegranate seeds, to garnish

Preheat the oven to 180°C/gas mark 4. Mix ½ tablespoon tahini with the pomegranate molasses and tamari or soy sauce in a medium bowl. Add the broccoli florets and thoroughly coat. Transfer to a lined baking tray and roast for 8–10 minutes. Keep a close eye to make sure they don't burn.

Heat the oil in a medium saucepan and sauté the onion, garlic, carrot, ginger, chilli flakes and broccoli stalks for 3–4 minutes. Add a splash of water if the vegetables stick to the pan. Add the cannellini beans and stock, bring to the boil and simmer for about 10 minutes, or until the carrot is tender.

Blitz the soup, with the remaining tablespoon of tahini, and season to taste. Serve garnished with the roasted broccoli, and a scattering of fresh pomegranate seeds.

roasted aubergine and wild rice

It is easy to find both Camargue and wild rice in supermarkets and health-food shops. Both are delicious grains of rice, much tastier and more satisfying, I think, than white and brown varieties. To mix them go for an 8:2 ratio of Camargue to wild. Some supermarkets do the work for you and sell it in packs already mixed.

Serves 4

Carbs 36g   Sugar 17g   Protein 6g   Fibre 6g   Fat 4g   Sat Fat 3g   Salt 1.4g

4 medium tomatoes on the vine, roughly chopped

2 stalks of lemongrass, roughly chopped

5 spring onions, roughly chopped

1 red chilli, deseeded if you prefer milder spice

30g ginger, peeled and roughly chopped

2 garlic cloves, peeled

juice of 1 lime

1½ tablespoons tamari or light soy sauce

850ml coconut water

100g mix of Camargue and wild rice

2 aubergines (approx. 500g)

1 tablespoon coconut oil

1 teaspoon cumin powder

salt and pepper

15g coriander, roughly chopped

Blitz the tomatoes, lemongrass, spring onions, chilli, ginger, garlic, lime juice and tamari or soy sauce until as smooth as possible. A blender is best for this – if using a hand-held stick blender blitz for a good few minutes.

Transfer to a saucepan, along with the coconut water and 200ml water. Bring to the boil. Meanwhile, wash and rinse the rice. Add to the simmering liquid and cook for 25 minutes with the lid on. Some froth may rise to the surface from the paste and the rice – simply skim this off.

Preheat the oven to 200°C/gas mark 6. Cut the aubergines into 2cm cubes. Melt the coconut oil if solid and pour over the aubergines, mixing well. Transfer to a large baking tray and season with the cumin powder, salt and pepper. Roast for about 25 minutes, turning halfway through and keeping a close eye to make sure they don't burn.

When ready remove from the oven, check for seasoning and stir through the chopped coriander. Serve soup with a handful of aubergine placed on top.

Not suitable for freezing

beetroot with tarragon buckwheat

Beetroot can take a ferociously long time to cook, so I grate it prior to cooking to allow the heat to penetrate much quicker, enabling this soup to be whizzed up in no time. As it is a fruit seed rather than a grain, buckwheat is gluten-free. It is also high in protein and soluble fibre, requires no overnight soaking and cooks in no time!

Serves 4

calories 147 · DF · GF · V · VE

Carbs 27g   Sugar 9g   Protein 4g   Fibre 4g   Fat 1.5g   Sat Fat 0.2g   Salt 0.3g

75g raw or unroasted buckwheat
generous pinch of salt
1 teaspoon olive oil
1 medium onion, roughly diced
1 garlic clove, finely sliced
½ teaspoon fennel seeds, ground in a pestle and mortar
3 medium beetroots, approximately 400–450g unpeeled weight
1 tablespoon plus 1 teaspoon sherry vinegar
750ml vegetable stock
28g tarragon, leaves picked and roughly chopped
1 teaspoon English mustard
black pepper

Rinse the buckwheat in a sieve under cold water and transfer to a saucepan with about 150ml cold water and a generous pinch of salt. Simmer with the lid on for 8–10 minutes until tender. Drain, and run under cold water to stop the cooking process. Set aside in the sieve to ensure all excess liquid drains from the seeds.

Gently heat the olive oil and add the onion, garlic and ground fennel along with 1 tablespoon water. Sweat, with the lid on, for 5 minutes, stirring regularly. Add a splash more water if the onion sticks to the pan.

Peel and coarsely grate the beetroots and add to the saucepan with the tablespoon of sherry vinegar and stock. Bring to the boil, reduce to a simmer and cook for 15–20 minutes, until the beetroot is tender.

Meanwhile pound the tarragon, mustard and teaspoon of sherry vinegar in a pestle and mortar to a smooth paste. Season to taste and stir through the buckwheat. Set aside.

When the soup is ready, blend until smooth and season to taste. If the beetroot is particularly sweet, a good grinding of pepper may be needed to create a good balance. Serve the soup, topped with the tarragon dressed buckwheat, and Beetroot Crisps (page 45).

aromatic dhal with mustard seeds and curry leaves

Sri Lanka gave me some of my most memorable food experiences. Dining in local hole-in-the-wall style restaurants I ate rice and curry almost every day. It was always served with Dhal and I was fascinated by the levels of flavour and texture in a dish made with something as basic as lentils. This recipe includes many ingredients, which can be intimidating, but you will not be disappointed.

Serves 4

Carbs 38g Sugar 5g Protein 17g Fibre 5.5g Fat 2g Sat Fat 0.2g Salt 0.1g

125g yellow lentils
125g red lentils
1 cinnamon stick
3 cardamom pods
2 cloves
1 onion, thinly sliced
3 garlic cloves, finely chopped
1 tablespoon coconut oil
½ teaspoon each of turmeric, ground cumin, ground cinnamon and garam masala
20g fresh ginger, peeled and grated
1–2 green bird's eye chillies, finely chopped
3 medium tomatoes, roughly chopped
1 tablespoon mustard seeds
20–25 curry leaves
lime wedges, to serve

Rinse the lentils under cold water until the water runs clear. Place in a saucepan with the cinnamon stick, cardamom pods and cloves and cover with 500ml cold water. Bring to the boil, cover and simmer for 25–30 minutes, stirring occasionally. If necessary, add some water while cooking, but only a little at a time.

Meanwhile, gently fry the onion with the garlic in ½ tablespoon coconut oil and 1 tablespoon water. Cook for 10–15 minutes, stirring regularly, until browned and caramelised, adding a splash more water if necessary. Add the ground spices, followed by the ginger, chillies and tomatoes. Cook until the tomatoes have broken down and surrendered their juices – about 10 minutes. Use a potato masher to break up any remaining chunks.

Remove the spices from the lentils, and beat or whisk for a few minutes to a smooth soup consistency, adding a little more water or stock if it is too thick. Pour in the spiced tomato mixture and stir through. Wipe the frying pan clean, add the remaining coconut oil, followed by the mustard seeds and curry leaves. Fry, stirring, until the mustard seeds begin to pop. Stir through the soup and serve with lime wedges.

courgette and feta puy lentil with black olives, capers and cherry tomatoes

While driving around Santorini with my husband, we'd stop to sample local dishes in shabby little restaurants. In the scalding heat, we ate mostly salads, effortlessly thrown together and bursting with the freshest ingredients, including juicy tomatoes, feta cheese, capers and olives, all locally grown.

This recipe aims to capture the beauty of the flavours I fell in love with there. You can buy cooked ready-to-eat puy lentils in supermarkets – they are a great store-cupboard standby and can be added to all kinds of soups.

Serves 4 calories 170 GF (V/VE if using vegetable stock)

Carbs 15g   Sugar 7.5g   Protein 10g   Fibre 5.7g   Fat 6g   Sat Fat 3g   Salt 0.5g

1 medium onion, finely chopped
1 garlic clove, finely chopped
½ tablespoon olive oil
3 large courgettes (approx. 1kg), peeled and cubed
750ml vegetable or chicken stock
60g feta cheese
120g cooked puy lentils
4 pitted black olives, finely chopped
1½ teaspoons capers, roughly chopped
8 cherry tomatoes, quartered

Sauté the onion and garlic in the olive oil and 1 tablespoon water for about 5 minutes until slightly softened. Add the courgettes and the stock, bring to the boil, reduce to a simmer and cook for 15–20 minutes.

Remove from the heat, crumble the feta cheese into the stock, then blitz until smooth. Return to the heat, add the cooked puy lentils and bring back to the boil. Serve garnished with black olives, capers and cherry tomatoes.

turkey and black quinoa with peas and basil

Just like chicken, turkey can be a little bland. But I like to see it as a blank canvas — something to enhance with the ingredients you add to it. Black quinoa has a wonderful nutty flavour and crunchy texture and, teamed with some fresh herbs, converts these meatballs into something truly special.

Serves 4

Carbs 15g   Sugar 3.8g   Protein 24g   Fibre 5g   Fat 6g   Sat Fat 1g   Salt 1g

65g black quinoa
250g turkey mince (thigh or breast)
3 sprigs of thyme, leaves picked
2 sprigs of basil (about 10 leaves), finely chopped
1 sprig of marjoram, leaves picked and finely chopped
1 spring onion, finely chopped
1 tablespoon tomato purée
¾ teaspoon salt
½ teaspoon black pepper
1 tablespoon olive oil
1 litre chicken or vegetable stock
250g frozen peas
25g basil leaves, roughly torn

Place the quinoa in a sieve and rinse under cold water. Transfer to a small saucepan, cover with 140ml water, add a pinch of salt, bring to the boil and cook with the lid on for 10–12 minutes. Remove from the heat and leave undisturbed for 5 minutes so that the grains absorb any water left in the saucepan. Return to the sieve, and run under cold water again to cool it completely. Squeeze out as much moisture as you can.

Mix the cooked quinoa with the turkey, thyme, basil, marjoram, spring onion, tomato purée, salt and pepper, until everything is evenly combined. Shape the mixture into 20 meatballs, roughly 20g each or the size of a golf ball. Refrigerate for 10 minutes to solidify. This step can be done in advance, and the meatballs frozen, if desired.

Place a large heavy-based frying pan or casserole dish on a medium heat with 1 tablespoon olive oil. Fry the meatballs on all sides until lightly browned, taking care not to burn them. Add the stock, bring to the boil and simmer for 7 minutes. Add the peas and cook for a further 3 minutes. Season to taste and stir in the basil just before serving.

watercress with balsamic beetroot-roasted chickpeas and parsley crab

This is my staple watercress soup recipe, made all the more special by the addition of roasted chickpeas and decadent crab. This one is a show stopper!

Serves 4

Carbs 21g   Sugar 11g   Protein 18g   Fibre 7.5g   Fat 7g   Sat Fat 1g   Salt 0.7g

For the chickpeas
250ml beetroot juice
1 tablespoon balsamic vinegar
1 x 400g can chickpeas, drained, rinsed and dried
salt and pepper

For the soup
½ small leek, finely chopped
1 garlic clove, chopped
1 celery stick, roughly chopped
1 large courgette (approx. 250g), roughly chopped
½ tablespoon olive oil
550ml vegetable or chicken stock
3 sun-dried tomatoes
100g fresh white crabmeat
few sprigs of parsley or tarragon, finely chopped
squeeze of lemon juice
350g watercress
375ml unsweetened soya milk

To make the chickpeas, place the beetroot juice and balsamic vinegar in a small saucepan and bring the boil. Simmer for 20–25 minutes, until the liquid has reduced to about 50ml, and has a thick syrupy consistency.

Preheat the oven to 200°C/gas mark 6. Place the chickpeas in a small baking tin, and pour over half of the syrup, mixing well. Season and roast for 10 minutes. Remove from the oven, pour over the remaining syrup and roast for a further 10–15 minutes, keeping an eye to make sure the syrup does not burn. When ready, set aside.

Sauté the leek, garlic, celery and courgette in the olive oil and 1 tablespoon of water for about 5–8 minutes. Add a splash more water if necessary. Pour in the stock, then the sun-dried tomatoes. Bring to the boil and simmer for 15 minutes.

Mix the crabmeat with the chopped parsley or tarragon, season with salt, pepper and a squeeze of lemon juice. Refrigerate until needed.

Remove the sun-dried tomatoes then add the watercress and soya milk. Simmer for a couple of minutes to soften. Blitz until smooth, and season to taste. Serve, topped with a spoonful of crabmeat and a scattering of chickpeas.

superfood soups

This chapter champions known superfoods, and includes recipes jam-packed with ingredients such as avocado, spinach, chia seeds, quinoa and coconut — all ingredients known to be particularly high in vitamins and antioxidants. It also looks at how a collection of ingredients can be combined into a dish that is truly powerful.

The Hangover Soup is inspired by a good, old-fashioned fry-up; it takes the healthier, more nutritious elements and presents them in a rehydrating and comforting soup. The Purity Soup, as its name suggests, tastes and feels thoroughly pure, and is a fantastic detox. A soup for breakfast may seem strange, but the breakfast bowls in this chapter are anything but. Full of ingredients that give you long-lasting, slow-releasing energy, they are a great way to start the day. The beautifully tart Chilled Rhubarb, Orange and Chia Seed Soup is served with a scoop of naturally sweetened Ginger and Vanilla Frozen Yogurt and makes a sophisticated and satisfying dessert.

These soups are designed to pack a nutritional punch — they are about as feel-good as food can be.

carrot, coconut and ginger with coriander sambal

Carrot and coriander is a soup classic. Here, I have simply taken inspiration from the essence of these ingredients and presented it in a slightly different way. Coconuts are simple to crack open, but can also be bought ready prepared in supermarkets.

Serves 4   (V/VE if using vegetable stock)

Carbs 17.1g   Sugar 13.4g   Protein 3.1g   Fibre 10.9g   Fat 14g   Sat Fat 11g   Salt 0.2g

100g fresh coconut, grated
½ teaspoon cumin seeds
½ teaspoon coriander seeds
2 shallots, diced
1 garlic clove, roughly chopped
50g ginger, peeled and grated
½ teaspoon chilli flakes
½ tablespoon coconut oil
650–700g carrots
750ml vegetable or chicken stock

Coriander Sambal
35g coriander, roughly chopped
25g grated fresh coconut
10g ginger, peeled and grated
1 small green chilli, deseeded and
   roughly chopped
juice of 1 lime
salt and pepper to season

If using a whole coconut, prepare it by piercing the three eyes with a skewer, and drain out the liquid. Then, wrap it in a towel, place on a hard surface, such as the floor (or take it outside) and give it a firm blow with a hammer to crack it open. Use a spoon to gently lift the flesh away from the harder exterior and remove the brown skin using a potato peeler if desired.

Toast the cumin and coriander seeds in a small frying pan for about 2 minutes, then grind in a pestle and mortar.

Sauté the shallots, garlic, ginger, chilli flakes and ground spices in the coconut oil and 1 tablespoon water for about 5 minutes, stirring occasionally. Add a splash of water if the mixture sticks to the pan.

Add the carrots, fresh coconut and stock. Bring to the boil and simmer for 30–35 minutes until the carrots are soft.

To make the sambal, place the coriander, grated coconut, ginger and chilli into a mini food processor and blitz to a rough, dry paste. Stir in the lime juice and season to taste.

When the soup is ready, blend until smooth, season and serve topped with the sambal.

purity soup with citrus-cured salmon, avocado, pink grapefruit and watercress

When I first made this soup, it occurred to me how pure it tasted, and so it acquired its name. The addition of fresh citrus flavours, creamy avocado and peppery watercress make it deliciously refreshing too. You could serve the salmon garnish in little baby gem lettuce leaves instead if you wish. In summer months, this soup is excellent chilled and served with the garnish as a salad on the side. It doesn't retain its bright green colour for very long, so best to serve it as soon as possible.

Serves 4 calories 225

Carbs 16g   Sugar 13g   Protein 9g   Fibre 6g   Fat 12g   Sat Fat 3.5g   Salt 0.2g

For the garnish
1 pink grapefruit, halved
juice of 1 lime, plus a little extra
   lime or lemon for the avocado
1 teaspoon agave syrup
80g salmon fillet
½ ripe avocado, diced
small handful of watercress leaves

For the soup
1 small onion, roughly chopped
30g ginger, grated
2 garlic cloves, chopped
1 Granny Smith apple, cored and
   diced
½ tablespoon coconut oil

Firstly, make the citrus-cured salmon. Squeeze the juice from 1 half of the grapefruit, combine with the lime juice in a small bowl and whisk in the agave syrup. Slice the salmon into very thin strips and add to the curing juice. Make sure it's covered, and refrigerate for 30 minutes.

Remove the segments from the remaining grapefruit half as neatly as possible. Chop each segment into thirds. Dice the avocado half and dress with a little lime or lemon juice to preserve its colour.

To make the soup, sauté the onion, ginger, garlic and apple in the coconut oil and 1 tablespoon of water for 10–15 minutes on a low heat, stirring regularly. Add a splash more water if necessary.

900ml vegetable stock

150g kale, any tough stalks removed

100g spinach

1½ ripe avocados (use the leftover half from the garnish)

10g parsley

zest of 1 and juice of ½ lemon

Add the stock and bring to the boil before adding the kale, followed by the spinach. There will seem like a vast quantity of leaves for the amount of liquid used, but they will wilt into the boiling stock very quickly. Encourage this by pressing them down with a spoon or spatula.

Simmer for 5–7 minutes. Remove from the heat and leave to cool a little, then add the avocado, parsley, lemon zest and juice. Blend immediately to retain the vibrant colour.

Divide the soup between 4 bowls. Pour away the curing juice and place the salmon on top of the soup, followed by the grapefruit, diced avocado and some watercress leaves. Serve immediately.

hazelnut, cranberry and chia seed oatcakes

These are a perfect accompaniment and delicious spread with nut butter and topped with a few slices of banana to stave off any sweet cravings. The delicate sweetness from the cranberries makes them a tasty snack in their own right.

Makes 24   calories 45   DF V VE

Carbs 5g   Sugar 0.8g   Protein 1.5g   Fibre 0.8g   Fat 2g   Sat Fat 0.2g   Salt 0.3g

40g blanched hazelnuts

150g jumbo oats

½ teaspoon bicarbonate of soda

1 teaspoon flaked sea salt

1 tablespoon hazelnut butter

Preheat the oven to 150°C/gas mark 2 and line a baking tray with parchment. Place the hazelnuts in a dry frying pan over a medium heat and toast until golden brown. Leave to cool a little before chopping roughly.

In a food-processor, blitz 100g of the jumbo oats, the bicarbonate of soda and salt to a fine powder. Add the

100ml boiling water
25g dried cranberries,
    roughly chopped
1 teaspoon chia seeds

hazelnut butter and pulse a few times to incorporate. Slowly add the water and stop mixing as soon as you have a sticky paste. Finally, add the hazelnuts, dried cranberries, chia seeds and remaining jumbo oats and pulse a few times until everything is just combined.

Tip out onto a clean surface and gather the mixture together into a firm ball. Place between two sheets of parchment paper and roll out to 3mm thickness. Remove the top piece of parchment and cut out 24 oatcakes using a 5cm round cutter. Transfer to the lined baking tray and bake for 30 minutes until golden brown. Leave to cool on a wire rack. They will keep for up to a week in an airtight container.

spinach, oat and hazelnut milk soup

The oats are multifunctional in this recipe, imparting their goodness and creating a creamy consistency to thicken the soup. It may sound odd, but it works and is a clever way to introduce a slow-burning grain into a meal that is not just porridge. This soup is the most electrifying green colour — almost too pretty to eat!

Serves 4

Carbs 17.5g   Sugar 6g   Protein 4.5g   Fibre 4g   Fat 4g   Sat Fat 0.6g   Salt 0.5g

½ small leek, roughly chopped
1 celery stick, roughly chopped
½ tablespoon olive oil
30g jumbo oats
500ml vegetable or chicken stock
400g spinach, rinsed and
  drained
250ml hazelnut milk (soya or
  almond milk will also work)
1 teaspoon freshly grated nutmeg
a handful of fresh basil
salt and pepper

Sauté the leek and celery in the olive oil and 1 tablespoon water for about 5 minutes, until softened. Stir in the oats, followed by the stock. Bring to the boil and simmer for 5 minutes. Add the spinach; if you are using a large saucepan, all the spinach may fit, otherwise add it in batches, allowing each batch to wilt before adding more.

Simmer for a couple of minutes to soften the spinach slightly. Add the hazelnut milk, nutmeg and basil. Blitz until smooth (a high-powered blender works best here). Season to taste, adding a touch more nutmeg if necessary. Bring to just below boiling point before serving.

Serve with Hazelnut, Cranberry and Chia Seed Oatcakes (page 135).

eat-the-rainbow vegetable broth

Serving these wonderful ingredients virtually uncooked preserves all of their natural goodness, vibrant colour and texture. The name comes from its colourful appearance, and falls in line with many health recommendations suggesting that our diet includes fruits and vegetables that, quite literally, resemble the colours of the rainbow.

Serves 4

Carbs 26g   Sugar 11g   Protein 19g   Fibre 7g   Fat 4g   Sat Fat 0.8g   Salt 0.5g

70g mixed wild rice (I used
   Camargue and wild rice)
80g Turmeric and Lemongrass
   Paste (page 18)
500ml coconut water
80g edamame beans
60g shiitake mushrooms,
   or 4 medium mushrooms
   (1 per bowl)
200g purple sprouting broccoli
2 medium carrots, julienned
2 spring onions, finely sliced
4 small radishes, finely sliced
5g nori, finely sliced
160g fresh tuna, thinly sliced
10g black sesame seeds

Cook the rice according to packet instructions. When ready, strain, run under cold water to stop the cooking process and set aside.

Gently sauté the Turmeric and Lemongrass Paste on a low heat to release all the flavour. Add the coconut water, along with 900ml water and bring to the boil. Simmer for 15 minutes. When ready, strain through a muslin-lined sieve (or use a clean J-cloth) and return to a clean saucepan. Season to taste and bring to a gentle simmer.

Add all the vegetables, cooking just long enough to heat them through, about 2–3 minutes.

Place the rice in the bowls, cover with the broth and vegetables. Top with the nori, fresh tuna and sesame seeds and serve immediately.

the hangover soup

This soup does for a hangover what chicken soup does for the common cold. Marmite and Worcestershire sauce add salty notes while Tobasco sauce introduces some spice to cleanse from the inside out. Rehydrating, comforting and nutritious - a whole new kind of cure!

Serves 4

Carbs 17.7g   Sugar 6.8g   Protein 10g   Fibre 7.7g   Fat 1.5g   Sat Fat 0.4g   Salt 1.7g

400g cherry tomatoes
1 tablespoon Tabasco sauce, plus
    extra to serve
salt and pepper
1 small onion, halved and
    thinly sliced
1 garlic clove, finely chopped
3 tablespoons Worcestershire
    sauce
250g portobello mushrooms,
    roughly chopped
750ml beef stock (or use
    Mushroom Stock, page 16,
    to make vegetarian)
400g canned haricot beans,
    drained and rinsed (240g
    drained weight)
1 teaspoon Marmite
small bunch of parsley, roughly
    chopped

Preheat the oven to 240°C/gas mark 9. Place half of the cherry tomatoes in a small roasting dish with the Tabasco sauce, a pinch of salt and a generous grinding of pepper. Roast for 15 minutes.

Sauté the onion and garlic on a low heat in 1 tablespoon of Worcestershire sauce and 2 tablespoons water, stirring regularly to prevent them catching and burning. Add more water if necessary. After about 10 minutes, when nicely browned and caramelised, add the mushrooms and remaining tomatoes and cook for a further 3–4 minutes. Add the stock and haricot beans, bring to the boil and cook for 15–20 minutes.

Season with the remaining Worcestershire sauce and the Marmite, and pepper if needed. Serve topped with the Tabasco-roasted tomatoes, some chopped parsley and Tabasco sauce on the side for an added kick!

superfood chowder

Soya milk has a beautiful, delicate flavour, and makes this soup rich and creamy without being overly calorific. It also boasts a whole array of benefits, being rich in omega-3 and 6, high in protein and fibre, essential fatty acids, vitamins and minerals. Furthermore, it contains mostly unsaturated fat with zero cholesterol. A worthwhile addition to any diet!

Serves 4

Carbs 22.5g   Sugar 7g   Protein 22g   Fibre 4.6g   Fat 6g   Sat Fat 0.8g   Salt 1.1g

100g black quinoa

pinch of salt

350ml unsweetened soya milk

250g undyed smoked haddock

1 bay leaf

1 onion, peeled and halved

6 peppercorns

1 medium leek, finely sliced

1 garlic clove, chopped

½ tablespoon olive oil

1 fresh corn on the cob

750ml vegetable stock

150g spinach, finely shredded

10g chives, finely chopped

Place the quinoa in a sieve and rinse under cold water. Transfer to a small saucepan, cover with 140ml water, add a pinch of salt, bring to the boil and cook with the lid on for 10 minutes. Remove from the heat, and leave undisturbed for 5 minutes, so that the grains absorb any remaining water. Return to the sieve, and run under cold water again to cool completely. Set aside until needed.

Place the soya milk in a medium saucepan with the smoked haddock, bay leaf, onion halves and peppercorns. Slowly bring to the boil and simmer for 3 minutes. Remove from the heat, and leave to stand, covered, for 5 minutes. Strain and set the cooking broth aside.

Clean the saucepan, and return to the heat. Sauté the leek and garlic in the oil and 1 tablespoon water on a low heat for about 5 minutes, until soft and translucent. Stand the corn upright and slide the blade of a sharp knife along the length of the cob, removing the kernels as you do so. Add these to the saucepan, along with the reserved cooking broth and vegetable stock. Add the cob for added flavour. Bring to the boil, immediately reduce to a simmer and cook for 7–10 minutes. When ready, remove the cobs and use a slotted spoon to skim any scum that has formed on the surface.

Add the cooked quinoa, along with the spinach and fish. Bring to just below boiling point, season to taste, garnish with some chopped chives and serve immediately.

spiced root vegetable soup

This bejewelled soup belongs in the centre of a table, shared by family and friends. Many of the spices used are known for their metabolism- and immunity-boosting properties. If you are serving up a feast, I recommend throwing together some Buckwheat Tortillas (pages 99–100). A loaf of Pumpkin Seed and Prune Rye Soda Bread (page 32) would be good to mop up the juices and some Vegetable Crisps (pages 45–47) would be delicious.

Serves 6   (if using vegetable stock)

Carbs 22g   Sugar 11g   Protein 3.5g   Fibre 6g   Fat 2g   Sat Fat 0.3g   Salt 0.2g

1 red onion, sliced

1 garlic clove, finely chopped

2 medium carrots, peeled and cut into 2cm cubes

½ tablespoon olive oil

¼ teaspoon chilli flakes (optional)

¼ teaspoon cayenne pepper

¼ teaspoon turmeric

½ teaspoon cinnamon

¾ teaspoon ground ginger

¾ teaspoon garam masala

1 medium sweet potato, peeled and cut into 2cm cubes

1 large parsnip, peeled and cut into 2cm cubes

1.2 litres vegetable or chicken stock

250g vacuum-packed cooked beetroot, cut into 2cm cubes, juice reserved

100g baby spinach, finely shredded

salt and pepper

40g coriander, roughly torn

Sauté the onion, garlic and carrots in the olive oil and 1 tablespoon water for about 5–8 minutes, until the onion is soft. Add the spices, mix well and cook for a minute or so. Add the sweet potato, parsnip and stock. Bring to the boil and simmer for 20 minutes. Don't be tempted to allow the soup to simmer untimed or unwatched. It is important to cook the vegetables until they are just tender, otherwise they will fall apart.

Add the beetroot, its juice and the spinach. Taste for seasoning, and stir through the coriander just before serving. Alternatively, you could pile the coriander on top of the soup if serving to a table of guests to create a bit of drama!

chilled avocado and wasabi with black sesame seed and nori booster

This recipe is quite rich, so a little goes a long way. To introduce some texture, serve topped with fresh slices of raw or seared tuna or even try a ceviche, curing some raw tuna in a little lime juice, salt and pepper, and serving it atop some Hoisin Sesame Seed Wonton Crisps (page 58).

Serves 4

calories 274

DF GF V VE

Carbs 7.5g   Sugar 5g   Protein 7g   Fibre 6g   Fat 23g   Sat Fat 6g   Salt 0.2g

For the black sesame seed and nori booster
1 sheet nori
1 tablespoon black sesame seeds

For the soup
2 shallots, roughly chopped
2 garlic cloves, roughly chopped
25g ginger, peeled and roughly chopped
1 teaspoon coconut oil
3 medium ripe avocados (approx. 350g when prepared)
juice of 2 limes
200g silken tofu
2 teaspoons wasabi paste
1 teaspoon white pepper
generous pinch of salt
300ml coconut water

Preheat the oven to 200°C/gas mark 6 and place the nori on a baking tray. Bake for 5 minutes until curled and crisp – it burns quickly, so keep an eye on it. Leave to cool, then blitz into small flakes. Add the sesame seeds and set aside.

Sauté the shallots, garlic and ginger in the coconut oil and 1 tablespoon water for 5 minutes, until softened. Be sure they don't catch and burn.

Slice the avocados in half, remove the stone and scoop out the flesh. Dress with a little lime juice to prevent them from browning. Transfer to a blender, along with the tofu, wasabi, lime juice, white pepper and salt. Add the sautéed onions, garlic and ginger, along with the coconut water and blitz until smooth.

Chill in the fridge for a couple of hours and serve garnished with a sprinkling of the black sesame seed and nori booster.

Note: this soup is best eaten on the day it is made, as it doesn't keep its beautiful pastel green colour or fresh flavours for long.

Not suitable for freezing

black rice, banana and coconut breakfast bowl

Black rice has high levels of fibre, meaning it is absorbed at a slower rate into the body keeping you feeling fuller for longer. Rarely would we be making breakfast for four, so this recipe serves two. If you are cooking for one, it will keep in the fridge until the following morning.

Serves 2

Carbs 50g   Sugar 16g   Protein 4.5g   Fibre 1.7g   Fat 4g   Sat Fat 3g   Salt 0.4g

80g black glutinous rice
½ teaspoon cinnamon
¼ teaspoon ground ginger
1 slice fresh ginger
250ml coconut water
1 banana, sliced or other fruit of
　your choice
30g pomegranate seeds
　(optional)
100ml unsweetened fresh
　almond milk
2 tablespoons coconut milk
a few mint leaves, to garnish

Soak the rice overnight. When ready to cook, rinse thoroughly, transfer to a small saucepan, with the spices, ginger, coconut water and 100ml cold water. Bring to the boil, cover with a tight-fitting lid or tinfoil and simmer for 30–35 minutes.

Prepare the banana and pomegranate seeds. When the rice is cooked, add the almond milk and bring back to the boil. Simmer for a couple of minutes, then remove the ginger. Divide between 2 bowls and top with fruit and coconut milk. Garnish with mint leaves and serve.

Not suitable for freezing

A note on black glutinous rice

This is the unprocessed whole grain of traditional sticky white rice. Nutty in flavour, chewy in texture and a vibrant burgundy colour when cooked, it is high in fibre, iron, copper, zinc and carotene, and packed with powerful antioxidants. It is lower in calories and carbohydrate than white and brown rice and higher in protein. Have a look in your supermarket, but you are more likely to find it in health-food shops and online.

chilled rhubarb, orange and chia seed soup

I have done little here to mask the beautiful tart flavours of rhubarb. Just a touch of agave syrup for sweetening, while roasting also helps to concentrate the natural sugars. Chia seeds are rich in omega-3 and high in protein and iron, making them a great little store-cupboard standby. This soup is as decandent a dessert as any.

Serves 4

calories 47 · GF · V

Carbs 6g Sugar 5g Protein 1.7g Fibre 3.3g Fat 0.9g Sat Fat 0.1g Salt 0g

For the consommé

600g fresh pink rhubarb, cut into 2cm cubes

zest and juice of ½ orange

1 star anise

seeds of ½ vanilla pod (reserve other half for Ginger and Vanilla Frozen Yogurt on page 152)

1 tablespoon agave syrup or honey

1 bay leaf

2 teaspoons chia seeds

Ginger and Vanilla Frozen Yogurt, to serve

mint leaves, to garnish (optional)

Preheat the oven to 180°C/gas mark 4 and place the rhubarb, orange zest and juice, star anise, vanilla seeds and pod, agave syrup, bay leaf and 150ml water into a shallow roasting tin. Cook for 30 minutes, until the rhubarb is soft and breaks up easily. Leave to cool, remove the aromatics, and then use the back of a soup ladle to press as much of the rhubarb as possible through a sieve. You should have about 100g rhubarb pulp left over – set this aside to make the Ginger and Vanilla Frozen Yogurt.

Give the soup a little whisk and chill for 2–3 hours, or overnight. This can all be done a day ahead and can be frozen if you are using a glut of rhubarb from the garden.

When ready to serve, stir 1 teaspoon chia seeds through the soup, and divide between 4 bowls. Top with a scoop of Ginger and Vanilla Frozen Yogurt, garnish with the remaining chia seeds, and a few small mint leaves if you have them.

Tip: It is nice to serve this soup in shallow glasses that have been cooling in the freezer.

ginger and vanilla frozen yogurt

This frozen yogurt is totally sugar free, gaining its sweetness from succulent golden sultanas. The fresh ginger cuts through the creamy yogurt and the vanilla brings the whole thing together to produce a decadent dessert. This recipe makes a small quantity, but it is easy to double up if you fancy making more.

Serves 4

Carbs 9g   Sugar 8.5g   Protein 3g   Fibre 0.8g   Fat 4g   Sat Fat 2.5g   Salt 0g

40g golden sultanas
150g full-fat Greek yogurt
25g ginger, peeled and very finely grated
100g rhubarb pulp (see page 151)
seeds of ½ vanilla pod (reserved from Chilled Rhubarb Soup on page 151)

Place the sultanas in a small saucepan and cover with 60ml of water. Bring to the boil and simmer for about 5 minutes. Take off the heat, leave to cool and then blitz to a smooth purée.

Add the Greek yogurt, ginger, rhubarb pulp and vanilla seeds and blitz for a few second more until nice and smooth.

Place in a small Tupperware tub and freeze. After a couple of hours, whizz the frozen yogurt in a small food-processor to remove any ice crystals, then return to the freezer. Repeat once more after another 2 hours. When ready to serve, leave to stand at room temperature for 10–15 minutes to allow it to soften slightly.

breakfast oat smoothie bowl done two ways

These two recipes are based on the idea of a smoothie, but made a lot more substantial by the addition of some beautiful garnishes that transform it into the kind of breakfast which will set your day off on a high. Hugely adaptable depending on what fruit you may have in your fridge, and what nutty seedy garnishes you have access to, these recipes are very much open to interpretation.

Blackberry Oat Smoothie Bowl with Berry, Seed and Lime Zest Garnish

Serves 2 calories 299 DF V VE

Carbs 46g   Sugar 26g   Protein 8g   Fibre 10g   Fat 7g   Sat Fat 0.9g   Salt 0.2g

50g jumbo oats, 1 tablespoon set aside for toasting
½ tablespoon chia seeds
2 small bananas
150g frozen blackberries, or fresh with 4 ice cubes
2 pitted soft prunes
5g fresh ginger, grated
250ml unsweetened almond or soya milk
pinch of cinnamon

For the garnish
40g raspberries
30g blueberries
30g blackberries
5g golden linseeds
5g pumpkin seeds
lime zest

Place the oats (minus 1 tablespoon), chia seeds, banana, blackberries, prunes, ginger and almond or soya milk in a blender and blitz until smooth. Toast the remaining jumbo oats in a dry frying pan over a medium heat, until golden. Dust with a pinch of cinnamon and set aside.

Divide soup between 2 bowls and serve garnished with the berries, seeds, toasted oats and a sprinkling of lime zest.

Mango, Tofu and Coconut Oat Smoothie Bowl with Chia Seeds, Kiwi and Passion Fruit

Serves 2 | calories 264 | DF | V | VE

Carbs 42g | Sugar 26g | Protein 8.5g | Fibre 8g | Fat 5g | Sat Fat 0.9g | Salt 0.2g

40g jumbo oats

1 medium mango, peeled (approx. 250g prepared weight)

100g silken tofu

¼ teaspoon ground turmeric

10g fresh ginger, peeled and grated

½ tablespoon agave syrup

150ml coconut water

zest of ½ and juice of 1 lime

1 kiwi, peeled and sliced

1 passion fruit, seeds scraped out

5g chia seeds

1 sprig of mint

Place the oats, three quarters of the mango, the tofu, turmeric, ginger, agave syrup, coconut water, lime zest and juice in a blender with 4 ice cubes and blitz until smooth.

Serve garnished with the remaining mango, kiwi, passion fruit, chia seeds and mint.

Not suitable for freezing

suppliers

Living in central London, I am surrounded by shops selling almost every ingredient I could possibly imagine. However, coming from a small town in Ireland, I am aware that unusual ingredients are not always that easy to find. The internet is the perfect solution and can easily become your local supermarket. I use it a lot for buying dry-store, Asian and other unusual ingredients, and for the odd online grocery shop when I am strapped for time. However, nothing can replace being able to see, touch and smell fresh ingredients, so I would always recommend buying fruit, vegetables, meat and fish from your local shops.

Asian ingredients

These suppliers sell a wide variety of Asian ingredients, including miso pastes, tofu, bonito flakes and kombu for Japanese dashi, gochujang, nori and konnyaki shirataki noodles:

www.souschef.co.uk

www.japancentre.com

www.clearspring.co.uk

www.theasiancookshop.co.uk

Spices

www.thespicery.co.uk

www.seasonedpioneers.co.uk

Mexican

You will find ancho chillies here, as well as fresh tomatillos when in season. They only sell dried hominy, but Sous Chef (see 'Asian ingredients') sells cooked hominy in cans.

www.coolchile.co.uk

Online grocery shopping

Many of the unusual ingredients in this book can be found on Ocado, so worth checking it out:

www.ocado.com

Store-cupboard essentials

These websites are fantastic for grains, pulses, flours and oils, among other things:

www.goodnessdirect.co.uk

www.realfoods.co.uk

index

A

almond milk 13, 30–1, 148–9, 153
asparagus 52–3
umami broth with five-spice
     asparagus, pork and chive
     dumplings 66–8
aubergine and wild rice 119
avocado 109–11
chilled avocado and wasabi with black
     sesame seed and nori booster
     146–7
purity soup with citrus-cured salmon,
     avocado, pink grapefruit and
     watercress 132–5

B

banana 148, 153
black rice, banana and coconut
     breakfast bowl 148–9
basil 30–1, 52–3, 72–3, 85–7, 124–5
beef
     beef stock 15
     pea and mushroom rare beef broth
        62–3
beetroot 144–5
     beetroot, chive and sumac
        buckwheat tortillas 99
     beetroot crisps 45
     beetroot with tarragon buckwheat
        120–1
     golden beetroot, fennel and
        saffron with poached rainbow
        trout 24–5
     watercress with balsamic beetroot-
        roasted chickpeas and parsley crab
        126–7
bisques 70–1
black bean, roasted tomato, harissa
     and pomegranate 113
blackberry oat smoothie bowl with
     berry, seed and lime zest garnish 153
blenders 8
bones 16
bonito flakes 17
bread, pumpkin seed and prune rye
     soda 32–5, 80
breadcrumbs
     panko 28
     savoury 35
broad bean, freekeh and smoked
     mackerel 114–15
broccoli
     broccoli and ginger with yogurt,
        cucumber and mint 96–7

cannellini bean with pomegranate
     and tahini-roasted broccoli 118
broths 49–55, 59, 62–3, 65–8, 81,
     84, 92–3, 138–9
bruschetta (rye), roasted cherry
     tomato 80
buckwheat
     beetroot with tarragon buckwheat
        120–1
     buckwheat tortillas done three ways
        99–101
     spiced consommé with salmon,
        buckwheat noodles and kale 69
butternut squash, miso roasted 26–7

C

cannellini bean, pomegranate and
     tahini-roasted broccoli 118
carrot 59, 144–5
     carrot, coconut, and ginger with
        coriander sambal 130–1
     carrot, rhubarb and yellow lentil
        106–7
cavolo nero, pearl barley and
     caramelised onion 116–17
celeriac with horseradish, lemon and
     parsley 40–1
celery, fennel, and cucumber broth
     with coriander, mint and lime
     pesto 92–3
chia seeds 134–5, 150–1, 154–5
chicken
     chicken stock 15
     fresh veg pot with soy broth
        chicken and pickled ginger 81
     Greek chicken and lemon with
        dill 112
     green vegetable broth with pistou
        chicken skewers 52–3
     Mexican posole verde 109–11
chickpea
     roasted red pepper, chickpea and
        herb 88–9
     watercress with balsamic beetroot-
        roasted chickpeas and parsley
        crab 126–7
chives 56–7, 66–8, 99
chowder, superfood 142–3
coconut (fresh), carrot and ginger
     with coriander sambal 130–1
coconut milk 70–1, 148–9
coconut oil 12
coconut water 12, 50–1, 70–3, 96–7,
     119, 138–9, 146–9, 154–5

consommés 49, 69, 72–3, 150–1
coriander 42–3
coriander, mint and lime pesto 92–3
coriander sambal 130–1
courgette 52–3, 100, 126–7
     chunky courgette and dill with
        prawns 102–3
     courgette and feta puy lentil with
        black olives, capers and cherry
        tomatoes 123
crab, watercress with balsamic
     beetroot-roasted chickpeas and
     parsley crab 126–7
crackers
     health-kick 108
     soda bread 34
cranberry, hazelnut, and chia seed
     oatcakes 134–5
crisps
     hoisin sesame seed wonton 58
     vegetable 45–7
croutons 34, 59
cucumber 72–3
     broccoli and ginger with yogurt,
        cucumber and mint 96–7
     chilled cucumber, almond and
        lemon 30–1
     fennel, celery and cucumber broth
        92–3

D

dashi, Japanese 17, 44, 64
dhal, aromatic dhal with mustard
     seeds and curry leaves 122
dumplings 65–8

E

edamame 12, 62–3, 138–9
     five-spice edamame relish 36–7
egg 90–1, 112
egg drop soup 94–5
equipment 8–9

F

fennel 24–5, 84, 92–3
feta
     courgette, feta cheese and thyme
        buckwheat tortillas 100
     courgette and feta puy lentil with
        black olives, capers and cherry
        tomatoes 123
five-spice 36–7, 66–8
fladelsuppe (German pancake soup)
     60–1

food intolerances 10
freekeh, broad bean and smoked
 mackerel 114–15
freezing food 9, 10
full-fat foods 10

G
ginger 81, 96–7, 130–1
ginger and vanilla frozen yogurt
 150–2
gochujang 12, 54–5, 90–1
 salmon and veg noodle pot with
  Korean gochujang broth 84
gorgonzola and lettuce with basil 85
granita 72–3
granola, savoury 108
grapefruit (pink), citrus-cured
 salmon, avocado, watercress and
 purity soup 132–5

H
haddock (smoked), superfood
 chowder 142–3
hangover soup, the 140–1
harissa, roasted tomato and
 pomegranate black bean 113
hazelnut, cranberry and chia seed
 oatcakes 134–5
hazelnut milk 13
 spinach, oat and hazelnut milk
  soup 136–7
herbs 10
hoisin sesame seed wonton crisps 58
hominy 13, 109–11

I
ingredients 10, 11–13

J
Jerusalem artichoke, thyme and
 mustard-roasted Jerusalem
 artichoke and garlic with red
 grapes 29

K
kale 69, 81–4, 132–4
kimchi with tofu 90–1
kombu 17

L
lemon 30–1, 40–1, 112
lemongrass
 sweetcorn, lemongrass and
  turmeric 38–9
 turmeric and lemongrass paste
  18–19, 38–9, 70–1, 138–9
 turmeric and lemongrass shellfish
  bisque 70–1

lentil 122
 carrot, rhubarb and yellow lentil
  106–7
 courgette and feta puy lentil with
  black olives, capers and cherry
  tomatoes 123
lettuce and gorgonzola with basil 85
lime 22–3, 42–3, 50–1, 92–3
low-fat foods 10

M
mackerel (smoked), broad bean and
 freekeh 114–15
mandolins 9
mango 72–3
 mango relish 50–1
 mango, tofu and coconut oat
  smoothie with chia seeds, kiwi
  and passion fruit 154–5
mint 86–7, 92–3, 96–7
miso 12, 62–3
 miso roasted squash 26–7
 miso soup with tofu and spring
  onions 64
 parsnip and walnut miso soup 44
 walnut, miso and spring onion
  tortillas 99
 walnut miso noodle broth with
  fennel, radish and enoki
  mushrooms 84
 walnut miso paste 18–19, 44,
  84, 99
mushroom 56–7, 66–8, 138–9, 140–1
 braised wild mushroom broth 59
 mushroom soup with a kick 98
 mushroom stock 16, 63
 pea and mushroom rare beef broth
  62–3
 walnut miso noodle broth with
  fennel, radish and enoki
  mushrooms 84

N
noodles 12
 lunch noodle pots 81–4
 spiced consommé with salmon,
  buckwheat noodles and kale 69
nori 13
 black sesame seed and nori booster
  146–7

O
oat(s) 108
 hazelnut, cranberry and chia seed
  oatcakes 134–5
 smoothie bowls 153–5
 spinach, oat and hazelnut milk
  soup 136–7

onion (caramelised), pearl barley and
 cavolo nero 116–17
orange, rhubarb, and chia seed
 chilled soup 150–1

P
pak choi 56–7, 62–3, 81
pancake soup, German 60–1
parsnip 144–5
 parsnip and walnut miso soup 44
 Sriracha parsnip crisps 45
passion fruit 72–3, 154–5
pastes 18–19, 38–9, 44, 70, 84, 99, 138
pea
 pea, mint and basil 86–7
 pea and mushroom rare beef broth
  62–3
 turkey and black quinoa with peas
  and basil 124–5
pearl barley, caramelised onion and
 cavolo nero 116–17
pesto, coriander, mint and lime 92–3
pistou 52–3
pomegranate 42–3, 72–3, 113, 118,
 148–9
pomegranate molasses 13, 113
pork
 umami broth with five-spice
  asparagus, pork and chive
  dumplings 66–8
 wonton soup 56–7
posole verde 109–11
prawn
 chunky courgette and dill with
  prawns 102–3
 prawn dumplings 65
 turmeric and lemongrass shellfish
  bisque 70–1
 wonton soup 56–7
pumpkin seed 108
pumpkin seed and prune rye soda
 bread 32–5, 80
purity soup 132–3

Q
quinoa, black 12, 142–3
 turkey and black quinoa with peas
  and basil 124–5

R
radish 62–3, 84, 109–11
rainbow trout, golden beets, fennel
 and saffron 24–5
red pepper 72–3
 roasted red pepper, chickpea and
  herb 88–9
 Sichuan-roasted red pepper with
  five-spice edamame relish 36–7

relishes 36–7, 50–1
rhubarb
  carrot, rhubarb and yellow lentil
    106–7
  chilled rhubarb, orange and chia
    seed soup 150–1
rice 138–9
  aubergine and wild rice 119
  black rice, banana and coconut
    breakfast 148–9

S
salmon
  purity soup with citrus-cured
    salmon, avocado, pink grapefruit
    and watercress 132–5
  salmon and veg noodle pot with
    Korean gochujang broth 84
  spiced consommé with salmon,
    buckwheat noodles and kale 69
sambal, coriander 130–1
sea bream, coconut and lime broth
  50–1
seasoning soups 10
sesame oil, toasted 13
sesame seed, black 12, 108, 138–9
  crispy sesame tofu fingers 28
  hoisin sesame seed wonton crisps
    58
  sesame seed and nori booster
    146–7
shellfish bisque, turmeric and
  lemongrass 70–1
smoothie bowls 153–5
soured cream, citrus 22–3
soy sauce 13
soya milk 13, 116–17, 126–7, 142–3,
  153
special dietary requirements 10
spices 10
spinach 132–5, 142–3, 144–5
spinach, oat and hazelnut milk soup
  136–7
Sriracha parsnip crisps 45
steak tartare, Korean (yukhoe), in
  broth 54–5
stock 9, 14–17
storing soup 9
sugar-snap pea 52–3, 62–3
sumac 13, 42–3, 99
sweet potato 42–3, 144–5
  peppered crisps 47
  sweet potato, sumac, pomegranate,
    peanuts, coriander and lime
    42–3
sweetcorn 142–3
sweetcorn, lemongrass and turmeric
  38–9

T
tahini-roasted broccoli and
  pomegranate with cannellini bean
    118
tofu 13, 146–7
  crispy sesame tofu fingers 28
  Korean kimchi with tofu 90–1
  mango, tofu and coconut oat
    smoothie with chia seeds, kiwi
    and passion fruit 154–5
  miso soup with tofu and spring
    onions 64
tomatillos 13, 109–11
tomato 36–7, 42–3, 52–3, 69, 88–9,
  119, 122, 140–1
  blackened tomato and Ancho chilli
    with citrus soured cream 22–3
  courgette and feta puy lentil with
    black olives, capers and cherry
    tomatoes 123
  the quickest tomato soup 78–9
  roasted cherry tomato rye
    bruschetta 80
  roasted tomato, harissa and
    pomegranate black bean 113
  tomato consommé cooler 72–3
tomato, sun-dried 67, 127
tortillas three ways 99–101
tropical consommé with granita 72–3
turkey and black quinoa with peas and
  basil 124–5
turmeric
  sweetcorn, lemongrass and
    turmeric 38–9
  turmeric and lemongrass paste
    18–19, 38–9, 70, 138
  turmeric and lemongrass shellfish
    bisque 70–1

U
umami broth with five-spice
  asparagus, pork and chive
    dumplings 66–8

V
vanilla and ginger frozen yogurt
  150–2
vegetables
  eat-the-rainbow vegetable broth
    138–9
  green vegetable broth with pistou
    chicken skewers 52–3
  salmon and veg noodle pot with
    Korean gochujang broth 84
  spiced root vegetable soup 144–5
  vegetable crisps 45–7
  vegetable stock 15

W
walnut
  parsnip and walnut miso soup 44
  walnut miso noodle broth with
    fennel, radish and enoki
    mushrooms 84
  walnut miso and spring onion
    tortilla 99
  walnut miso paste 18–19, 44,
    84, 99
wasabi and avocado 146–7
watercress
  purity soup with citrus-cured
    salmon, avocado, pink grapefruit
    and watercress 132–5
  watercress with balsamic beetroot-
    roasted chickpeas and parsley
    crab 126–7
wonton crisps, hoisin sesame seed 58
wonton soup 56–7

Y
yogurt 96–7
  ginger and vanilla frozen yogurt
    150–2
yukhoe in broth 54–5

acknowledgements

Writing a cookbook has been a dream of mine for a very long time and the reality came about as a result of much support, encouragement and belief from my family, friends and people I have been very lucky to encounter along the way.

To my Mum, and Dad who is sadly no longer alive, thank you for encouraging me to explore my passion for cooking – even though you had just put me through four years of fashion college. Mum, thank you for all the endless hours we spend on the phone, for your infinite wisdom and advice. My brothers Mark and Gary, sisters Liz and Grace, thank you for always believing in me.

There were many tasters employed to help me develop the recipes in this book. Kate, Ciara and Freda, the team at Propeller, my family, my husband and his gorgeous family, thank you all for lending me your tastebuds. There were two in particular, whose help and never-ending love of soup helped me to refine many of the recipes in this book. Mikey and Sammy, I love you for loving soup as much as you do and for being such wonderful friends.

My journey from kitchens and managing bakeries to food styling came about because a very special lady, Annie Rigg, took a chance on me after I pestered her with numerous emails asking her to give me a job. I have spent many happy years assisting Annie (and walking Mungo) and she has taught me everything I know. You are inspiration personified and a cherished friend.

An incredible team of people have worked on this book. Liz Belton, I was blown away by the props you chose – I couldn't have loved them more. Laura Edwards, as always your talent is insurmountable. Annie Rigg, your magic touch flows through each and every page. Louise Leffler you have brought it all together to create a book I feel so proud to be a part of. I cannot thank you all enough for bringing my ideas to life.

I feel incredibly lucky and honoured to be writing my first book for Kyle Books, such an esteemed publishing house. A million thank you's for giving me this opportunity. A big thank you also to Claire, my editor. You have been endlessly patient and helpful – I have so enjoyed our journey together.

To my little daughter Elsie. Thank you for being the angel you are and bouncing happily in your bouncer while I finished this book.

And finally, to Rich, my husband and best friend – you are the most amazing person I have ever met. I am so lucky to have you. Thank you for loving me, even though I made you eat soup for six months!